Sheila Thorne

Entertaining
Complete menus for all occasions

Cookery adviser: Jane Grigson

Entertaining

Complete menus for all occasions

Anne Willan

English edition by Elisabeth Evans

Book Club Associates, London

Good food begins at home and for this I thank my
MOTHER AND FATHER
to whom I dedicate this book

Line illustrations by Patricia Ludlow
Colour photography by Bruce Pinkard

CONTENTS

Acknowledgement

The author wishes to thank the following for their cooperation in producing the colour photography for this book: the Waterford Crystal Centre for the loan of the beautiful crystal used in the photographs, Judy Hill for her excellent cooking, and Debra Rathbone, Didi Pinkard, Simon Tuite, Frances Jenkinson and Richard Coltart for their efforts behind the scenes.

INTRODUCTION

A French friend of mine – no stranger in the best
restaurants in Paris – used to insist that she ate better at
home than anywhere else. I thought she was joking until I
lived with her for six months and experienced her cooking
first hand. The brilliance was not just technical, although
she was an excellent cook; it was the care she lavished on
finding just the right ingredients, the accuracy with which
she chose the appropriate wine, and the ease with which
she organized all the preparations and brought everything
to the table on time, cooked just as she liked it, that made
such memorable meals.

Since I have been married I have tried to follow the same
path, carefully planning meals around well-tried favourites
that not only taste good, but can always be relied on to
succeed after the most taxing day at work or with the
children. Now I run a cooking school in Paris it will
scarcely be a surprise that most of my favourite recipes are
French in inspiration – lavish in their use of eggs and
cream, and often flavoured with plenty of wine and herbs.
However, few of them are complicated classics since, like
everyone who works and entertains at the same time, I do
not have days or even hours to spend on the menu.
Whenever possible, I like to prepare ahead, serving dishes
like *crêpes* (that can be reheated), and braising rather than
roasting when there is a choice. I always try to reserve the
precious last moments in the kitchen not for some routine
task, but to put the finishing touches to a soufflé, or add
just the right balance of seasoning to a sauce.

One blessing for the harassed cook is the freezer and I
never hesitate to use it. Many of the dishes in this book will
live happily in its confines for several weeks. As a general
rule, all baked goods – bread, cakes and pastry – freeze
perfectly, provided they do not have a creamy filling.
Unfortunately, anything creamy, whether a custard, sauce

or soup tends to separate if frozen. Meat and poultry in a sauce, coq au vin or braised beef, for instance, freeze well, though when they are plainly roasted they may dry out.

I have arranged this personal collection of favourite recipes as party menus – all easily interchangeable – with a countdown giving an hour-by-hour, minute-by-minute timetable for preparing and cooking every dish. Every party makes its own demands on your time, your skill and your patience but the introductions to each of the thirty-two menus include plenty of advice on how to cope with a variety of different situations. The menus cover every kind of occasion and are arranged in eight chapters for parties of two, four, six, eight, ten, twelve, twenty-four and fifty people. So start entertaining on whatever scale you like and turn to page 11 to choose your menu.

ANNE WILLAN   La Varenne
34 Rue St Dominique
75007 Paris

HOW TO USE THIS BOOK

1. Decide what kind of party you want to give. Is it for just a few friends or for large numbers? Are you planning a morning or evening occasion, stand-up or sit-down, elaborate or informal? What do your budget, your space, and the season permit?

2. Check the chapter in the *Contents* corresponding to the size of the party you plan. Maybe you'll discover a menu there that is exactly what you want, be it a winter lunch for six, a gourmet picnic for ten, a traditional buffet for twenty-four, or cocktail canapés for fifty. General information about these menus, and some suggested alternatives, are given in the introduction to each chapter.

3. If you still haven't found just what you want, turn to the *Menu Table* (page 11) where the thirty-two menus are organized by type of occasion – midday or evening, outdoor, formal, and so on. Perhaps you want to give a kebab party for a dozen friends; don't be deterred because the menu for the kebab barbecue serves twenty-four. *With every recipe in this book go instructions for increasing or decreasing quantities.*

4. Now turn to the menus that have caught your eye. Consult the introductions to each menu to learn more about the recipes – suggestions about special ingredients, possible substitutions, and unusual cooking techniques, with a bit of culinary history thrown in for good measure. Look at the *Countdown* to find out if the plan of work fits your own schedule – most allow for the maximum of advance preparation, but a few are designed for those hurried occasions when you have to do everything at the last minute. Then make your final choice of menu and glance through the recipes again to prepare a shopping list. Before you begin, remember that:

Recipe quantities are for average appetites and may need adjusting depending on your guests.

Dishes prepared in advance should always be kept in the refrigerator except when the *Countdown* indicates otherwise.

Reheating times in the *Countdown* are approximate since the size and type of pan and the temperature of ingredients vary considerably.

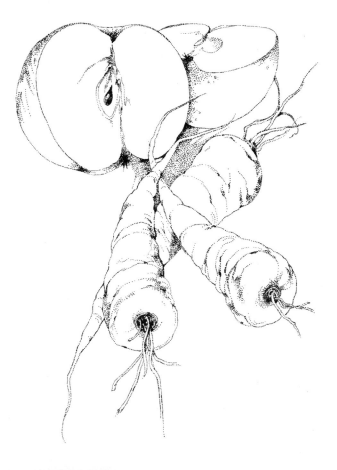

MENU TABLE

	For Two	For Four	For Six	For Eight	For Ten	For Twelve	For Twenty-Four	For Fifty	Ideal Outdoors	Formal Occasions	Stand Up or On Your Lap	Hearty Eating
Morning												
Hearty breakfast			●									●
Make-it-in-the-morning brunch						●			●		●	
Mid-day												
Patio lunch		●							●			
Summer lunch			●						●			
Winter lunch			●									●
Elegant lunch					●					●		
Fork lunch						●			●		●	
Outdoor lunch							●		●			
Evenings												
Six o'clock supper	●										●	
Fireside dinner	●										●	
Last minute supper		●									●	
Elegant dinner		●								●		
A quick supper			●								●	
Dinner outdoors			●						●			
Sophisticated supper				●								
Dinner for all seasons				●						●		
Dinner in a hurry					●							
Winter dinner						●				●		
Summer dinner						●			●	●		
Exotic cocktail party							●				●	
Kebab barbecue							●		●		●	
Cocktail canapés								●			●	
Single-plate supper								●			●	
Any time												
Plan ahead picnic	●								●		●	
Impromptu picnic	●								●		●	
Square meal		●										●
Summer buffet			●						●	●		
Gourmet picnic				●					●		●	
Winter buffet				●								●
Traditional buffet							●			●		
Feast of curry								●				●
Formal buffet								●		●		

MENUS FOR TWO

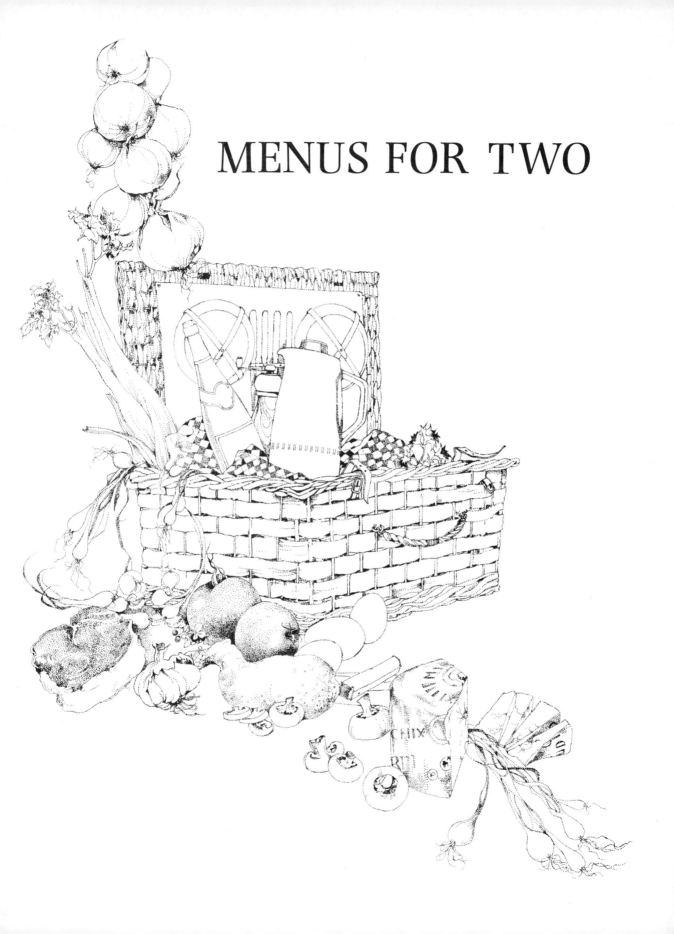

Fireside Dinner

Six O'Clock Supper

A Plan-Ahead Picnic

Impromptu Picnic

MENUS FOR TWO

Cooks complain that a simple menu for two can take almost as long to prepare as the same meal for four or even six people. But don't be discouraged – cooking for two has its advantages. With so few people to please, it is easy to plan the ideal menu for individual tastes. Little details of garnish and presentation will be doubly appreciated, whereas if they were served to a crowd they might pass unnoticed. And with few dishes and plates to remove after each course, you can serve the meal at your own pace, then relax and enjoy it.

A leisurely fireside dinner conjures up agreeable images of cold winter nights beside a log fire. A hearty steak, stuffed with mushrooms and served in a simple wine sauce, will complete the picture of cheerful comfort. This is the time to splurge on a good red wine; open it an hour or two before dinner so its flavour and bouquet develop to their best.

For an alternative menu for all year round, turn to the Elegant Dinner in Menus for Four. Any leftover green pea soup can be reheated to serve another time, and the stuffed orange recipe is easy to cut in half. To reduce the quantities of coq au vin simply make the recipe with a 1–1.2-kg, 2–2½-pound chicken, keeping the amounts of the remaining ingredients as stated.

A Six O'Clock Supper means time is of the essence. The menu of melon salad, baked pork chops, and clafoutis (a baked cherry pudding from the Limoges region of France) will take you easily to the theatre, the cinema, or out on the town since the recipes can be prepared ahead. If you are not able to do this, try halving the quantities for the Last-Minute Supper in Menus for Four. Everybody loves veal scaloppine and Marsala-flavoured zabaglione, and since the cooking times are short, this menu won't keep you away from your guest.

When you have a day outdoors in mind, a Plan-Ahead Picnic will give you the chance to rise at dawn with a delicious lunch all prepared to go. Or if you decide on the spur of the moment, the Impromptu Picnic offers devilled chicken legs and a hearty sandwich of eggs and sweet peppers, adapted from the pipérade of Spain's Basque country – both recipes can be made in a few minutes.

Fireside Dinner

Kipper Pâté with Hot Toast

Stuffed Steak Marchand de Vin

Fondante Potatoes

Syllabub

Now that hearty breakfasts seem to be found only in the novels of P.G. Wodehouse, another use has been found for the traditional breakfast kipper. Kippers make excellent pâté – their meat is rich and full of flavour, while any saltiness is counteracted by the cream and butter used in the recipe. The best kippers look firm and are never oily or dry; you can also find kippers ready-cooked in tins and plastic vacuum packs. If they seem too salty, a half-hour soak in milk may help.

The dessert of syllabub dates from mediaeval times, and is made with cream, whipped until thick with fruit juice, brandy, and wine. The name comes from sille, the Elizabethan word for wine from Champagne, and bub, meaning a frothy drink. In those days champagne was flat – the sparkling wine we know as champagne was not invented until the eighteenth century – so you can make syllabub with sauternes or any other sweet white wine and still be traditional. Syllabub looks most attractive in stemmed glasses. If you can find them in an antique shop, use the stemmed syllabub glasses with small handles made especially for this dessert. The flavour of syllabub improves on standing, so try to make it at least six hours in advance.

Innumerable little French restaurants serve steak *marchand de vin*, that brings out all the flavour of good steak, pan fried and served with a simple sauce made by dissolving the pan juices in red wine and adding a little garlic, shallot, and herbs. The herbs must be fresh, so use parsley and chives and add tarragon, basil, marjoram, and thyme in season. In the following recipe, the steaks have the extra touch of a stuffing of finely chopped mushrooms, called duxelles.

With the steak comes another French stand-by, fondante potatoes. Fondante means melting and the potatoes are fried in a covered pan so they cook in the butter and in their own steam until meltingly tender. Small new potatoes make the best fondante potatoes, but large ones, cut and shaped to resemble new small ones, can also be used.

17

COUNTDOWN

Day Before
Make pâté, cover and chill.
Make syllabub, cover and chill.

In the Morning
Make stuffing for steak.
Peel potatoes and keep in cold water.

1–2 Hours Ahead
Stuff steak; prepare ingredients for sauce.
Cook potatoes and leave in pan for
  reheating

Just Before Dinner
Make toast.

After Serving Appetizer
Reheat potatoes.
Cook steak and make sauce.

Kipper Pâté with Hot Toast

1 pair (about 450 g/1 lb) kipper fillets
1 cup/2.5 dl/$\frac{1}{2}$ pt milk
$\frac{1}{2}$ cup/125 g/$\frac{1}{4}$ lb butter, softened
3–4 tbs double cream
freshly ground black pepper
salt (optional)
thinly sliced white bread (for toast)

This quantity can be doubled, tripled, or
even made in four times this amount.

Put the kipper fillets in a baking dish, pour
over the milk, cover with foil and bake in a
moderate oven (180°C, Mark 4, 350°F) for
12–15 minutes or until the kipper flakes
easily. Let cool to tepid, drain and flake the
meat, discarding bones and skin, Mix half
the fish with half the butter and $1\frac{1}{2}$ tablespoons cream in a blender and work until
smooth, then blend remaining kipper,
butter, and cream. Add more cream, if
necessary, to make a pâté that just falls
from the spoon. Work in black pepper to
taste and a little salt if the pâté is bland.
Pile the pâté in a bowl or pack it in a dish
or ramekins and smooth the top. Cover and
chill.

   Just before serving, toast the bread, and
cut into fingers, trimming the crusts. Serve
the toast in a napkin so it stays hot.

Stuffed Steak Marchand de Vin

2 fillet steaks, cut $3\frac{1}{2}$ cm / $1\frac{1}{2}$ inches thick
$\frac{1}{2}$ tbs oil
salt and pepper
2 shallots, finely chopped
1 clove garlic, crushed
1.8 dl / 6 fl. oz / $\frac{3}{4}$ cup red wine
2 tsp chopped parsley
1 tsp chopped fresh herbs – chives, tarragon, basil, thyme, or marjoram
bunch watercress (for garnish)

For the duxelles
1 tbs butter
$\frac{1}{2}$ onion, finely chopped
175 g / 6 oz mushrooms, finely chopped
$\frac{1}{2}$ clove garlic, crushed (optional)
2 tsp chopped parsley

trussing needle and string

This recipe can be doubled or quadrupled, but it is hard to fry more than eight steaks at a time unless you are an expert.

Cut as large a pocket as possible in the steaks with a sharp knife.

For the duxelles: Melt the butter, add the onion and sauté over low heat until soft but not brown. Add the mushrooms and cook over high heat, stirring, until all the moisture has evaporated. Add the garlic, if used, and cook thirty seconds longer. Take from the heat and add the parsley with salt and pepper to taste.

Let the stuffing cool, then fill it into the steaks and sew them with a trussing needle and string.

A short time before serving, heat the oil in a heavy pan. Add the steaks and fry them over fairly high heat, allowing 2–3 minutes on each side for rare steak. Sprinkle the steaks with salt and pepper after turning. When they are done, transfer them to a platter, remove the trussing strings, and keep warm. Let the pan cool slightly, then add the shallots and garlic and cook gently for 1 minute. Add the wine and stir to dissolve the pan juices; simmer until the sauce is reduced by half. Add the parsley and other herbs, taste for seasoning and pour over the steaks. Garnish the dish with watercress and serve at once.

Fondante Potatoes

---

350 g/¾ lb small new potatoes or 2 large
  regular potatoes
50 g/2 oz/¼ cup butter
salt and pepper

You can double or triple this recipe; larger
amounts of potatoes are hard to brown
evenly.

Scrub new potatoes to remove the skin or
peel them with a vegetable peeler. Peel
regular potatoes, cut in quarters and trim
the edges with a peeler so the potatoes are
oval. In a shallow saucepan or flameproof
casserole, melt the butter and add the potatoes – *they all should touch the bottom of the
pan.* Cover tightly and cook over high heat
for 15–20 minutes until the potatoes are
tender, shaking the pan occasionally to turn
the potatoes; they cook in their own steam
and will brown evenly without burning. If
preparing ahead, reheat potatoes in the
same pan. Sprinkle with salt and pepper
before serving.

Syllabub

---

4 tbs sauternes or sweet white wine
2 tbs brandy
2 tbs lemon juice
85 g/3 oz/⅓ cup sugar
1.75 dl/6 fl.oz/¾ cup double cream
little ground nutmeg or cinnamon (for
  sprinkling)

This recipe can be doubled or tripled.

Mix the wine, brandy, lemon juice, and
sugar in a bowl and stir to partially dissolve
the sugar. Stir in the cream, then beat with
an electric beater for 1–2 minutes until
froth rises to the surface. Skim off the froth
with a large metal spoon and pour it into a
stemmed glass. Continue beating and skimming until only a little thin liquid is left.
Discard it or, if you like, add it to the glasses of syllabub – it will fall to the bottom.
Cover and chill at least 4 hours and up to
24 hours. Just before serving, sprinkle the
syllabub with ground nutmeg or cinnamon.

Six O'Clock Supper

Melon and Grape Salad
Pork Chops with Cheese
Baked Aubergine
Clafoutis Limousin

Supper should be simple, and few dishes are easier than melon and grape salad made with halves or quarters of melon, scooped into balls, and mixed with seedless green grapes. A cream dressing made with lemon juice and flavoured with fresh mint makes this an appetizer, but the same idea can be followed for dessert if the fruit is macerated in liqueur and sugar rather than dressing. Be sure to choose an orange-fleshed melon like cantaloupe or charentais to contrast well with the green grapes. If you like, you can add variety to the salad with peeled tomatoes and cucumber rings.

The recipe for pork chops with cheese is a Swiss favourite using Gruyère; the chops are baked slowly in white wine and stock, then topped with a cheese and onion mixture. At the same time, bake a dish of aubergine, browned first in olive oil, then topped with tomatoes seasoned with garlic; both these dishes can be prepared ahead.

Clafoutis comes from Limoges in south western France, a region famous for its cherries. The story goes that when the august body of the Académie Française decided to define the word clafoutis as a kind of fruit pie, the Limousins rose as one in protest, declaring that not only is clafoutis not a pie but it should be made only with one kind of fruit – tiny black cherries. They were so successful in their demands that the official dictionary definition of clafoutis now reads black cherry gâteau.

Gâteau is a fancy name for what in fact is a pudding made of crêpe batter baked in the oven with cherries and brandy. There is no reason why you should not make your own version with tart red cherries, fresh plums, apples, peaches, or any other tart fruit.

COUNTDOWN

Day Before
Cook pork chops, add cheese topping and
    keep covered.
Prepare aubergine and keep covered.

In the Morning
Make melon and grape salad.
Stone or drain cherries and leave in
    baking dish. Make batter, but do not
    add to dish.

45 Minutes Before Serving
Set oven at moderate (180°C, Mark 4,
    350°F).

30 Minutes Before Serving
Stir clafoutis batter, pour over cherries,
    add brandy or kirsch, and bake.
Reheat pork chops in oven.
Bake aubergine

Just Before Serving
Pile salad in melon shells.
Turn oven to low and keep pork chops
    and aubergine warm.
Take out clafoutis and leave in a warm
    place.

Melon and Grape Salad

1 small or $\frac{1}{2}$ medium cantaloupe or
    charentais melon
225 g/$\frac{1}{2}$ lb/1 cup seedless green grapes
1 tbs chopped fresh mint

For dressing
pinch of salt
2 tsp sugar
freshly ground black pepper
1 tbs lemon juice
1 tbs oil
2 tbs single cream

This salad can be made for as many people
as you like.

Cut the melon in half, if necessary, discard
the melon seeds and scoop out the flesh
with a ball cutter. Scrape the shell clean,
cut in quarters and chill. Mix the melon
balls in a bowl with the grapes.
    For dressing: Stir the salt, sugar, and a
little black pepper into the lemon juice until
dissolved. Whisk in the oil, followed by the
cream, so that the dressing emulsifies and
thickens slightly. Spoon the dressing over
the fruit, mix carefully until thoroughly
coated and taste for seasoning, adding more
salt, pepper, and sugar if necessary. Cover
and chill for up to 6 hours.
    Just before serving, add chopped mint to
fruit; pile in melon shells.

Pork Chops with Cheese

2 tbs oil
1 onion, chopped
4 medium (about 450 g/1 lb) loin pork
  chops
1.25 dl/$\frac{1}{4}$pt/$\frac{1}{2}$ cup white wine
1.25 dl/$\frac{1}{4}$pt/$\frac{1}{2}$ cup stock
salt and freshly ground black pepper
2 tbs fresh white breadcrumbs
2 tsp chopped parsley
100 g/$\frac{1}{4}$lb/$\frac{1}{2}$ cup grated Gruyère cheese

This recipe can be made easily for up to
eight people.

In a shallow casserole heat the oil and
sauté the onion over medium heat until soft
but not brown. Lift it out with a slotted
spatula and reserve. Add the pork chops to
the pan and brown them on both sides.
Pour over the wine and stock, sprinkle with
a little salt and pepper, cover and simmer
on top of the stove or bake in a moderate
oven (180°C, Mark 4, 350°F) for $\frac{3}{4}$-1 hour or
until the chops are very tender.
  Mix the breadcrumbs, parsley, reserved
onion, and Gruyère cheese, add a little
black pepper and stir in enough liquid from
the pork chops to bind the mixture. Spread
the mixture on the chops in the casserole
and grill them 3–4 minutes until browned.
  To prepare ahead: Cook the chops and
spread with cheese mixture. *To reheat them:*
Bake in a hot oven (200°C, Mark 6, 400°F)
for 15–20 minutes until hot and
browned.

Baked Aubergine

1 medium aubergine, sliced
salt and freshly ground black pepper
4 tbs olive oil
1 onion, chopped
2 medium tomatoes, peeled, seeded, and
  chopped (page 207) or 1 cup tinned
  tomatoes, crushed
1 clove garlic, crushed
1 bay leaf

This recipe can be made for any number of
people.

Sprinkle the aubergine with salt and leave
30 minutes to draw out the bitter juices.
Rinse with cold water and dry on paper
towels.
  In a pan heat 3 tablespoons of the oil and
sauté the aubergine until browned on both
sides. Arrange the slices, overlapping, in a
buttered shallow baking dish. Add remaining oil to the pan and sauté the onion until
soft but not brown. Add the tomatoes,
garlic, bay leaf, salt and pepper, and cook,
stirring occasionally, until the mixture is
pulpy. Spoon it over the aubergine, cover
the dish, and bake in a moderate oven
(180°C, Mark 4, 350°F) for 25–30 minutes
until the aubergine is tender; discard the
bay leaf. The dish can be prepared ahead
and baked just before serving, if you like.

Clafoutis Limousin

350 g/¾ lb/1½ cups tart cherries, stoned, or 1 tin (450 g/1 lb) stoned red tart cherries in water, drained.
50 g/2 oz/⅓ cup flour
pinch of salt
75 g/3 oz/⅓ cup sugar
2 eggs, beaten to mix
1.25 dl/¼ pt/½ cup milk
3 tbs brandy or 2 tbs kirsch
icing sugar (for sprinkling)

shallow baking dish (1½ l/3 pt capacity)

You can double or triple the quantities of clafoutis, but be sure to use a shallow baking dish.

Set the oven at moderate (180°C, Mark 4, 350°F) and butter the baking dish. Spread the cherries in the dish.

Sift the flour into a bowl with the salt, add the sugar, and make a well in the centre. Add the eggs with a little milk and gradually stir in the flour to make a smooth batter. Stir in the remaining milk. You can prepare the batter up to 6 hours ahead. Just before baking stir the batter and pour it over the cherries, spoon over the brandy or kirsch, and bake in the heated oven for 35 minutes or until the clafoutis is puffed and brown. Let cool to warm (the clafoutis will sink slightly) and sprinkle with icing sugar before serving.

A Plan-Ahead Picnic

Potted Ham and Beef
Cracked Wheat Bread
Tomatoes
Cheese-stuffed Celery
Sticks
Fresh Lemon Cake

Potted ham is a type of pâté packed in a pot or dish. Potted meats are cooked very slowly for a long time in a casserole whose cover is sealed with flour and water paste (luting paste) to retain the flavour. Then the mixture is minced, packed tightly in a pot – you could use a small casserole – to exclude all the air, and the surface is sealed with a layer of butter or fat. When carefully made, potted meats keep in a cool place for several weeks. Not surprisingly, they were

designed in the days before refrigeration to preserve meat throughout the winter and to relieve the monotonous diet of salt meat that was the rule on long sea voyages. This particular recipe calls for York ham, but any similar well-flavoured ham will do.

The chewy texture of cracked wheat bread, with its nutty flavour of whole wheat flour, is ideal with the pâté. More and more stores are selling stone-ground whole wheat flour and it is well worth a search. The same store will also probably have cracked wheat (sometimes called bulgur) which is a common ingredient in Middle Eastern dishes; it comes in several textures – coarse, medium, and fine. Like all homemade bread, cracked wheat bread is at its best when very fresh, and it becomes stale within a day. However, since it freezes perfectly, you can make the loaves ahead and keep them in the freezer until you need them.

Dessert is a fresh lemon cake, easy to carry if you simply leave it in the loaf pan. The ground peel of the lemon is added to the batter for a refreshing tang, and after it is baked, the cake is moistened with lemon juice.

The menu is rounded out with celery sticks stuffed with cheese and some tomatoes or any fresh vegetable you fancy.

Everyone is always thirsty outdoors, so don't forget plenty of drinks such as vacuum flasks of hot soup and coffee in winter or, in summer, chilled soft drinks and beer carried in a container of ice, insulated to beat the heat.

COUNTDOWN

1–2 Weeks Before
Make potted ham and beef and seal with
butter.
Make cracked wheat bread and store,
tightly wrapped, in freezer.

Day Before
Make fresh lemon cake, cool and wrap
tightly to carry.
Make cheese-stuffed celery sticks and
wrap.
Take bread from freezer and leave to
thaw.
Wipe tomatoes and pack in plastic box.
Chill drinks.

In the Morning
Pack potted ham and beef, bread, celery
sticks, tomatoes, and cake in picnic
basket. Put hot drinks in a vacuum
flask; pack cold drinks with ice in
insulated container.

Potted Ham and Beef

225 g/½ lb cooked or raw York ham, with
plenty of fat
225 g/½ lb rump or chuck steak
½ tsp ground allspice
½ tsp freshly ground black pepper
1.25 dl/¼ pt/½ cup water
salt (optional)
50 g/2 oz/¼ cup melted butter (to seal)

For luting paste
2 tbs flour
2–3 tbs water

*casserole with tight-fitting lid (7.5 dl/1½ pt/3-
cup capacity)*

Potted ham and beef can be made in
almost any quantity.

Cut the ham and beef in 2.5 cm/1-inch
cubes, discarding sinew but keeping the fat.
Put the meat in the casserole with the
spices and pour over the water. *The meat
should fill the casserole completely.*
To make the luting paste: Mix the flour
with just enough water to make a soft
paste; do not stir too much or the paste will
become elastic. Seal the gap between the
casserole and lid tightly with luting paste.
Bake the casserole in a low oven (150°C,
Mark 2, 300°F) for 3 hours. Let cool without removing the lid so the juices are
retained.
    Work the meat mixture through the
coarse plate of a mincer and taste for
seasoning; if the ham was salty, no more
salt will be needed. Pack the meat tightly
into 2 ramekins or small pots and pour the
melted butter on top to seal it.
    Potted meat easily keeps in the refriger-
ator for 2 weeks if the seal is not broken.
Carry it to the picnic in the ramekins or
pots.

Cracked Wheat Bread

1 package dry yeast or 1 cake compressed
   yeast, or 45 g/½ oz fresh yeast, or
   ¼ oz dried yeast
3.25 dl/¾ pt/1½ cups lukewarm water
350–400 g/12–14 oz/2–2½ cups strong white
   flour
125 g/¼ lb/1 cup stone-ground whole wheat
   flour
1 tsp salt
1 tsp sugar
50 g/2 oz/½ cup finely cracked wheat
1 egg white, beaten lightly (for glaze)

6 *small 12 cm × 6 cm × 4 cm, 4½ × 2½ × 1½ inch
   loaf pans or 1 medium 22 cm × 11 cm × 6 cm,
   8½ × 4½ × 2½ inch loaf pan*

This recipe can be doubled.

Grease the loaf pans. Sprinkle or crumble the yeast over the water and let stand 5 minutes or until dissolved. Mix 225 g/½ lb/2 cups strong white flour and the whole wheat flour in a bowl with salt, sugar, and cracked wheat, and make a well in the centre. Pour the yeast mixture into the well and mix with the hand to form a dough that is soft and slightly sticky. Turn the dough out on a well-floured board and knead for 5 minutes or until it is smooth and elastic, adding more flour if it sticks to the board. Put the dough in a greased bowl, turn it over so the top is greased and cover with a damp cloth. Let rise in warm, draught-free place for about 1 hour or until doubled in bulk.

Work the dough lightly to knock out the air, divide into 6 or keep in one piece and shape into loaves. Put in the loaf pans, cover with a damp cloth, and let rise again until almost doubled in bulk and the dough reaches the top of the pans. Set oven at moderately hot (190°C, Mark 5, 375°F). Brush with lightly beaten egg white (for a crisp crust) and bake in the heated oven, allowing about 30 minutes for the small loaves or 40 minutes for the larger ones or until the loaves sound hollow when tapped on the bottom. Brush the bread with egg white again during baking if you want a very crisp crust. Transfer to a rack to cool and keep in a plastic bag in the freezer until the morning of the picnic.

Cheese-Stuffed Celery Sticks

1 bunch celery
2 tbs milk
100 g/¼ lb Roquefort or other blue cheese
100 g/¼ lb/½ cup butter, creamed
freshly ground black pepper

This recipe is easy to make in large quantities.

Trim the celery and divide into sticks of even length. Bring the milk almost to the boil. Crumble the cheese into a bowl and beat in enough hot milk to make a smooth, soft mixture. Beat in the butter with black pepper to taste. Spread the cheese mixture down a stick of celery and press another stick, upside down, on top; the rounded sides form a cylinder. Wrap in foil. Fill and wrap the remaining sticks in the same way and chill thoroughly, preferably overnight.

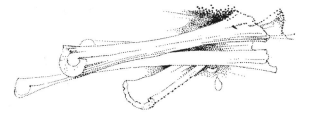

Fresh Lemon Cake

1 lemon
1 egg
125 g/¼ lb/1 cup flour
½ tsp salt
½ tsp bicarbonate of soda
50 g/2 oz/¼ cup butter
175 g/6 oz/¾ cup sugar
6 tbs milk
75 g/3 oz/½ cup sultanas
25 g/1 oz/¼ cup coarsely chopped walnuts

22 cm × 12 cm × 6 cm, 8½ × 4½ × 2½ inch loaf tin

Quantities of this cake can be doubled.

Grease the loaf pan and set the oven at moderate (180°C, Mark 4, 350°F). Squeeze the lemon and reserve the juice. Cut the lemon peel in large pieces and work it with the egg in a blender until puréed. Sift the flour with the salt and bicarbonate of soda.

Cream the butter, gradually beat in the sugar and continue beating until soft and light. Beat in the egg and lemon mixture. Stir in the flour mixture alternately with the milk in 2 batches. Stir in the sultanas and walnuts. Spoon the batter into the loaf pan and bake in the heated oven for 45–50 minutes or until the cake springs back when lightly pressed with a fingertip. Spoon the reserved juice over the cake while it is still warm and leave to cool in the pan. Wrap cake and tin in foil or a plastic bag to carry.

Impromptu Picnic

Pipérade in Syrian Pita Bread

Devilled Chicken Legs

Chilled Watermelon Slices

Pipérade in Syrian pita bread is an offbeat but excellent sandwich. By itself, pipérade is a Basque dish of scrambled eggs with sweet peppers and tomatoes, flavoured – in true Basque fashion – with plenty of garlic. Syrian pita bread, now available in many stores and some supermarkets, is a flat, soft round about 18cm/7 inches across, If you bake it a few minutes in the oven, then cut the rounds directly across, the two puffy semicircles form ideal pockets for filling.

If you have left no time for shopping, you will probably already have most of the ingredients for the pipérade eggs, tomatoes, and garlic. Vegetables like tinned mushrooms or leftover marrow, corn, or peas can be substituted for the peppers. Syrian pita bread is hardly a stock item, so a hollowed out French loaf can be used instead. As for the chicken, most people have a few pieces, whether dark or white meat, in the refrigerator or freezer. Already cooked chicken will need grilling in the devil mixture for only a few minutes; the raw pieces take a little longer.

Watermelon is always a refreshing end to a picnic, but if you don't have any on hand, or if it is out of season, substitute any other juicy fruit – some fragrant pears, for instance, or strawberries with a bowl of sugar for dipping. Add a bottle of chilled rosé wine or, in winter, a flask of hot soup, and you are ready to go.

COUNTDOWN

1 Hour Before Leaving
Chill the watermelon and drinks.
Make the tomato purée for the pipérade.
Make the devilled chicken legs and let
  cool.

30 Minutes Before Leaving
Finish the pipérade, stuff in Syrian pita
  bread and let cool.

Just Before Leaving
Wrap the chicken legs and pipérade in
  foil and pack in picnic basket.
Wrap melon in a plastic bag and pack
  with ice in insulated container; add
  cold drinks.
Put hot drinks in a vacuum flask.

Pipérade in Syrian Pita Bread

1 large or 2 small round Syrian pita breads

For the pipérade
2 tbs olive oil
1 small onion, thinly sliced
1 small tomato, peeled, seeded, and chopped
  (page 207)
2 cloves garlic, crushed
$\frac{1}{2}$ tsp marjoram
salt and freshly ground black pepper
$\frac{1}{2}$ red or green sweet pepper, cored, seeded,
  and diced
3 eggs, beaten to mix

You can make pipérade in double or triple
this quantity; served hot without bread, it is
an excellent snack or supper dish.

Set oven at moderate (180°C, Mark 4,
350°F).
  In a small pan heat the oil, add the
onion, and sauté over low heat until soft
but not brown. Add the tomato, garlic,
marjoram, and salt and pepper, and cook
gently, stirring occasionally, for 15 minutes
or until thick and pulpy; add the pepper
and cook 5 minutes more. Taste for seasoning.
  Bake the bread in the heated oven for 2
minutes until heated through. Cut it across
in half and slit each half with a knife to
form a pocket.
  Mix the eggs with salt and pepper and
stir into the tomato and pepper mixture in
the pan; cook, stirring constantly, until the
mixture thickens, as for scrambled eggs.

When it is almost thickened to your taste, take it from the heat – the mixture will continue to thicken in the heat of the pan. Spoon the hot mixture into the bread, let cool, then wrap in foil to carry.

Devilled Chicken Legs

4 raw or cooked chicken legs
1 tsp dry mustard
1 tsp French mustard
1 tsp Worcestershire sauce
pinch of cayenne
pinch of salt
2 tbs melted butter
100 g / $\frac{1}{4}$ lb / $\frac{1}{4}$ cup browned breadcrumbs

This is an easy recipe to make in quantity for large numbers of people, and a favourite barbecue stand-by.

Heat the grill. Score the chicken legs deeply with a pointed knife. Mix together the mustards, Worcestershire sauce, cayenne, and salt, and rub into the chicken meat, working the mixture well into the slits. Dip the legs in melted butter, then roll them in breadcrumbs.

For cooked chicken legs: Grill 3–4 minutes on each side or until browned.

For raw chicken legs: Grill 8–10 minutes on each side or until browned and tender. Let cool, then wrap in foil to carry.

Menus
for Four

An Elegant Dinner

A Square Meal

Patio Lunch

Last-Minute Supper

MENUS FOR FOUR

Cooking for four is a pleasure. Now is the time to branch out with new recipes – the gathering of family or friends is large enough to make experiments worthwhile but not too expensive. And there's no need to be formal. Everyone will be much more at ease if they feel free to come with you into the kitchen and poke in the pots and pans as well as discuss the food when it comes to the table. You may learn a lot from their comments – and they will certainly learn from you. As for wines, why not try that new bottle from Italy or bring out the vintage claret you have been keeping for an appeciative audience. Plan on two bottles to serve four.

All the recipes in the Elegant Dinner are offbeat. The colourful soup is made with fresh or frozen peas instead of the usual dried split peas. The coq au vin calls for white wine instead of red; the stuffed oranges contain the surprise of strawberry sherbet, concealed by a topping of crisp meringue.

A Square Meal of beef roulades in a red wine sauce, accompanied by baked barley, has the robust appeal of good country cooking. The country theme continues with the Danish dessert, peasant in a veil, which is an apple purée with grated chocolate and whipped cream.

Weather warm enough for a Patio Lunch calls for a cooling menu, and few appetizers are more appealing than chilled lemon soup, topped with a sprinkling of chives. Seafood pie and a dessert of fresh peaches baked in honey make the most of favourite summer ingredients. All these dishes can be prepared ahead, leaving you time to enjoy your guests and the sun.

Equally free of last-minute complications is the Light Summer Buffet in Menus for Eight. To adapt it for four, choose one of the two chicken dishes and halve the quantity of the rice salad. The walnut pastry left over when you make one instead of two peach flans is a bonus; roll it out thinly and bake it to serve as biscuits for another occasion.

But even if you haven't planned ahead, it is perfectly possible to produce a superb Last-Minute Supper in an hour or so. Your guests will feel complimented by food made to order – Caesar salad, followed by veal scaloppine and zabaglione. Or you may prefer to adapt the Quick Supper suggested in Menus for Six. The quantities for the baked scallops and saffron rice are easy to reduce, and you can make enough strawberries Romanoff for six and enjoy any left over the next day.

An Elegant Dinner

Fresh Green Pea Soup
Coq au Vin Blanc
Pilaf
Tomato and Watercress
Salad Vinaigrette Dressing
Oranges en Surprise

In the days when cooks depended on their gardens for a supply of fresh vegetables, fresh pea soup, made with the first fruits of the vegetable patch, was one of the treats of the spring season. Now you can enjoy its brilliant colour and fresh mint flavour all year since you can use fresh or frozen peas.

Any cook interested in French food has a recipe for coq au vin. But this one is different. It uses white instead of red wine,

and the resulting sauce is lighter and less inclined to overwhelm the elusive flavour of the modern chicken. Mass production and freezing have made the old-fashioned farm-yard fowl a wistful memory for most of us, but good plump chickens with plenty of fat under the skin to add flavour and richness to the meat do still exist. Fresh chickens are certainly worth every extra penny.

Rice is a weak point in the repertoire of many cooks – they complain it sticks to-gether no matter what they do – but rice pilaf is relatively foolproof. The rice is sautéed in butter before any liquid is added, and this coating of fat helps to keep the grains separate. As an added advantage rice pilaf reheats perfectly.

Oranges en surprise are a version of the famous baked Alaska, where ice cream is coated with meringue and baked briefly in the oven. In this recipe, hollowed orange shells are filled with fruit and ice cream, then capped with meringue. The only trick is to cover the ice cream completely so no heat can reach it. You can use any kind of sherbet or ice cream and any combination of fruits; a spoonful or two of liqueur im-proves their flavour. The result looks – and tastes – spectacular.

COUNTDOWN

Day Before
Make the soup but do not add the butter
    and cream; keep covered.
Make coq au vin and cover.
Cook pilaf and keep covered.
Make dressing for salad.

In the Morning
Peel and core tomatoes; wash water-
    cress.
Prepare fruit for oranges and leave to
    macerate.

45 Minutes Before Serving
Set oven at moderate (180°C, Mark 4,
    350°F).
Slice tomatoes and complete salad, but
    do not add watercress.
Make meringue for oranges.

30 Minutes Before Serving
Put chicken in oven to reheat.

15 Minutes Before Serving
Put pilaf in oven to reheat.
Reheat soup and add cream and butter.

After Serving Soup
Add watercress to salad.

After Serving Chicken
Complete oranges en surprise and bake.

Fresh Green Pea Soup

7.5 dl/1½pt/3 cups well-flavoured chicken
    stock (page 210)
2–3 sprigs fresh mint (optional)
salt and freshly ground black pepper
675 g/1½ lb fresh peas, shelled, or 1 package
    frozen green peas
1.25 dl/¼pt/½ cup double cream
2 tbs butter

You can make this soup in as large quantities as you wish. It is delicious served
chilled as well as hot.

Bring the soup to the boil, add half the
pepper to a boil, add the peas, cover and
simmer 5–8 minutes for frozen peas or
15–20 minutes for fresh peas, or until peas
are very tender. Discard the mint and purée
the mixture in a blender or work it through
a food mill. *You can prepare 24 hours ahead
up to this point.*
    Bring the soup to a boil, add half the
cream, and take from the heat. Stir in the
butter, a small piece at a time, and taste for
seasoning. Ladle the soup into bowls, add a
tablespoon of cream to each bowl and stir
to marble it.

Coq au Vin Blanc

18–20 baby onions
a 1½–2 kg/3½–4 lb roasting chicken
1 tbs oil
2 tbs butter
100 g/¼ lb piece bacon, diced
2 tbs flour
2.5 dl/½ pt/1 cup white wine
2.5–3.25 dl/½–¾ pt/1–1½ cups chicken stock
2 cloves garlic, crushed
2 shallots, finely chopped
bouquet garni
salt and freshly ground black pepper
225 g/½ lb mushrooms, quartered
1 tbs chopped parsley (for garnish)

Coq au vin blanc can easily be doubled or tripled; the flavour mellows if it is made a day or two ahead.

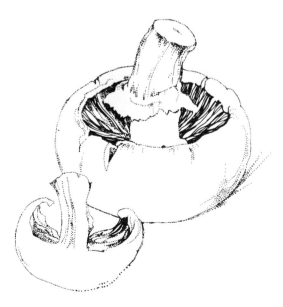

Set the oven at moderate (180°C, Mark 4, 350°F). Put the onions with their skins into boiling salted water, leave for 1 minute; drain and peel them. Cut the chicken into 6 pieces (see page 209).

In a heavy-based casserole heat the oil and butter and add the chicken, skin side down. Cook over medium heat until brown; turn over and brown the other side. Take out, add the onions and brown them also. Remove the onions, add the bacon and cook until well browned. Drain off all but 1 tablespoon of fat, add the flour and cook, stirring until brown. Pour in the wine, 1 cup/2.5 dl/½ pint stock, the garlic and shallots, bouquet garni, salt and pepper, and replace the chicken. Cover tightly and cook in the heated oven for 20 minutes. Replace the onions, stir gently to mix, cover and continue cooking 10 minutes. Add the mushrooms, stir again and add more stock if the sauce is thick. Cover and continue cooking 5–10 minutes until the chicken is very tender. Discard bouquet garni and taste for seasoning. *You can prepare 1–2 days ahead up to this point.*

To reheat: Put the coq au vin in a moderate oven (180°C, Mark 4, 350°F) for 20–25 minutes or on top of the stove until very hot. Sprinkle with chopped parsley and serve in the casserole.

Pilaf

---

3 tbs butter
1 onion, chopped
350 g/$\frac{3}{4}$ lb/1$\frac{1}{4}$ cups rice
6.25 dl/1$\frac{1}{4}$ pt/2$\frac{1}{2}$ cups stock or water
salt and freshly ground black pepper

Pilaf can be made in as large a quantity as
you have a pan to take it.

In a heavy-based casserole melt 2 tablespoons of the butter and sauté the onion
until soft but not browned. Add the rice and
cook about 2 minutes, stirring, until the
butter is absorbed and the grains look
transparent. Add the stock or water with
salt and pepper, cover and bring to the boil.
Simmer on top of the stove or cook in a
moderate oven (180°C, Mark 4, 350°F) for
exactly 20 minutes. *Let the pilaf stand,
covered, 10 minutes so the rice grains cool and
contract slightly.* Dot the top with remaining
butter, stir with a fork to fluff up the rice,
and taste for seasoning. *You can prepare
ahead up to this point.*

To reheat: Cook pilaf in a moderate oven
(180°C, Mark 4, 350°F) for about 15 minutes or heat it gently on top of the stove
until very hot.

Tomato and Watercress Salad

---

4 large ripe tomatoes, peeled, cored, and
    sliced (page 207)
1 bunch watercress
1 shallot, finely chopped
1 clove garlic, crushed (optional)
6 tbs vinaigrette dressing (see next recipe)

This salad can be made in any quantity you
wish.

Arrange the tomato slices, overlapping,
down one side of the four individual plates.
Mix the shallot and garlic, if used, with half
the vinaigrette dressing and spoon over the
tomatoes. Toss the watercress with the remaining dressing and arrange along the
other side of the plates.

Vinaigrette Dressing

Vinaigrette is the simplest of dressings, made basically with oil and vinegar, but its character can be changed to a startling extent by the kinds of oil and vinegar used and the seasonings added to them. For instance, you have a choice of tasteless vegetable oil, light peanut oil, or fruity olive oil; vinegars range from aromatic herb vinegars to wine vinegar to cider vinegar and obscure homemade brews. Lemon juice can be substituted for vinegar (in slightly smaller quantity) and is the choice of many wine connoisseurs who claim that vinegar spoils the taste of good wine. To the oil and vinegar you can add mustard (Dijon mustard is the best), garlic, or herbs (preferably fresh).

The final choice depends partly on what the dressing is for and partly on your personal taste. Delicate ingredients – salad, eggs, and fish, for intance – need a light dressing, but cooked vegetable salads or cold meats are enhanced by a hearty olive oil and full-bodied wine vinegar. The choice of seasonings – garlic, herbs, mustard, or just salt and freshly ground black pepper – is largely up to you.

This is the classic recipe for 4 tablespoons vinaigrette dressing: Whisk 1 tablespoon vinegar with $\frac{1}{4}$ teaspoon salt and $\frac{1}{4}$ teaspoon freshly ground black pepper until the salt is dissolved. Gradually whisk in 3 tablespoons oil until the dressing is slightly thickened and emulsified. Taste for seasoning. The dressing will separate on standing, but it will re-emulsify if you whisk it again. If you make large quantities of dressing in a screwtop jar, all you need do is shake it just before using.

Oranges en Surprise

4 large navel oranges
100 g / ¼ lb / 1 cup any mixed diced fruits –
    for example, strawberries, cherries,
    grapes, melon, pears, bananas
1 tbs sugar, or to taste
2 tbs Cointreau or Grand Marnier liqueur
    (optional)
2.5 dl / ½ pint strawberry or raspberry sher-
    bet, well frozen.

For the meringue
100 g / ¼ lb / ½ cup sugar
1.25 dl / ¼ pt / ½ cup water
2 egg whites
½ tsp vanilla

icing bag and medium star nozzle (optional)

Oranges en surprise are best made for eight
people or less because of the last-minute
assembly. For two, halve the quantities of
fruit and ice cream; you cannot, however,
make a smaller amount of meringue than
the portion called for here.

Cut a 1 cm / ½-inch slice off the tops of the
oranges and scoop out the flesh with a teaspoon. Discard as much pith as possible
and divide the flesh in chunks. Mix the
flesh with the chosen fruits, sugar to taste
and add liqueur, if used. Cut a thin slice off
bottoms of oranges if they do not sit firmly.
Pile the mixture into the orange shells, to
half-fill them, cover and chill. *You can prepare 6–8 hours ahead up to this point.*

*Not more than an hour or two before
serving, make the meringue:* Gently heat the
sugar and water until dissolved; bring to
the boil and boil steadily until the syrup
forms a thread between finger and thumb
when a little is lifted on a spoon. Meanwhile stiffly whip the egg whites. Add the
boiling syrup, beating constantly, and continue beating until the meringue is cool and
very thick. Stir in the vanilla. Leave
meringue in the bowl or put it in an icing
bag fitted with a star nozzle, if used, and
keep it in the refrigerator.

Just before serving, set the oven at very
hot (240°C, Mark 8, 450°F). Fill each orange
shell almost to the brim with sherbet. Cover
the sherbet completely with meringue,
using a spoon or the icing bag. *Take care to
seal the edges of meringue to the orange shells.*
Bake the oranges in the heated oven for 4–5
minutes so the meringue is lightly browned
but the heat has not penetrated to the
sherbet. Serve at once.

A Square Meal

Egg and Ham Mayonnaise

Braised Beef Roulades with Kidney

Baked Barley

Danish Peasant in a Veil

Egg mayonnaise with ham is just one of several simple appetizers you can make by combining hard-boiled eggs with that most popular of cold sauces, mayonnaise. For additional colour, dice a few cooked vegetables and mix them with mayonnaise to serve with the halved, hard-boiled eggs. An alternative to the ham could be strips of cooked chicken or cooked salmon, flaked with a fork. Preparation can be done ahead, but assemble the dish only a short time before serving because mayonnaise starts to dry out and discolour when left in the open air for more than an hour or so.

Baked barley, robust and chewy, is a fine foil for the richness of beef roulades stuffed with kidney. This recipe is a good example of the French talent for making gourmet dishes out of everyday ingredients. Rump steak and beef kidneys are simmered on a bed of vegetables in red wine, following the classic method for braising. Long slow cooking makes the meat almost tender enough to cut with a fork and the cooking juices are lightly thickened later to make a delicious sauce.

It is important that a braise be cooked slowly in even heat, and the traditional casserole, used in the days before ovens were commonplace in most kitchens, is called a braisière. It has a tight-fitting lid, indented to hold hot coals so that the pan can be heated from above as well as below. You can still buy these pans. For oven cooking, fill the indented lid with cold water. This makes the steam in the pan condense and fall back into the meat juices, so no flavour is lost by evaporation.

Danish peasant in a veil is less rustic than its name suggests. It is based on whole apples that are cooked to a pulp, the skins contributing all their flavour before the apples are puréed. Simmer the purée with spices and sugar until it is as thick as apple butter. Chill and dress with grated chocolate and whipped cream.

COUNTDOWN

2 or 3 Days Ahead
Make mayonnaise and keep covered.
Make apple purée and keep tightly
    covered.

Day Before
Hard-boil eggs and leave in shells; cook
    vegetables for salad.
Cook beef rolls and keep in casserole
    ready for reheating.
Bake barley.

1 Hour Before Serving
Whip cream and complete dessert.
Complete egg salad.
Chop parsley for beef.
Set oven at moderate (180°C, Mark 4,
    350°F).

30 Minutes Before Serving
Put beef rolls in oven to reheat.

20 Minutes Before Serving
Put barley in oven to reheat.

10 Minutes Before Serving
Turn oven to low to keep rolls and
    barley warm.
Make sauce for beef rolls.

After Serving Appetizer
Spoon sauce over beef rolls and sprinkle
    with parsley.

Egg and Ham Mayonnaise

2 carrots, diced
100 g/$\frac{1}{4}$ lb/$\frac{3}{4}$ cup diced cooked ham
175 g/6 oz/1 cup cooked green peas
2.5 dl/$\frac{1}{2}$ pt/1 cup mayonnaise (see page 45)
$\frac{1}{2}$ tsp Dijon mustard
3–4 tbs single cream
4 hard-boiled eggs
salt and freshly ground black pepper
little paprika (for sprinkling)

This recipe can easily be halved or increased in quantity.

Cook the carrots in boiling salted water for
8–10 minutes until tender and drain. Mix
them with the ham, peas, half the mayonnaise and the mustard; taste for seasoning.
Mix enough cream with the remaining
mayonnaise to give it the consistency to
coat the back of a spoon. Peel the hard-
boiled eggs and keep in cold water. *You can
prepare 6–8 hours ahead up to this point.*
    Not more than an hour before serving,
drain the eggs and dry well on paper
towels; *if they are damp, the mayonnaise will
slide off them.* Halve the eggs lengthwise and
arrange two halves, flat side down, on four
individual plates or set all the eggs, flat side
down, in a semicircle on an oval or circular
dish. With a large spoon, coat each egg
with mayonnaise. Pile the ham salad beside
the eggs on small plates or in the centre of
the semicircle on a large dish. Sprinkle the
eggs with a little paprika to add colour, and
serve.

Mayonnaise

Mayonnaise is made by beating oil into egg yolks so the mixture emulsifies, then flavouring it with vinegar. Like vinaigrette dressing, the flavour of mayonnaise depends on the oil and vinegar you use. Unless you are addicted to olive oil, you will probably prefer a lighter oil such as peanut. Most vinegar is fine for mayonnaise, provided it is not too harsh – the sharper the flavour, the less you will need.

Mayonnaise curdles easily, particularly in the early stages of mixing, so it is important, first, that all ingredients be at room temperature and, second, that the oil will be added very slowly until the mayonnaise starts to thicken, If it does curdle, try adding a tablespoon of boiling water and beating hard, If it still fails to thicken, you must start again, adding the curdled mixture drop by drop to a fresh egg yolk.

Mayonnaise can be kept for two or three weeks in an airtight container in the refrigerator. When it gets very cold it tends to separate, so if it has been stored for several days, let it come to room temperature before stirring.

This recipe makes about 2.5 dl$/\frac{1}{4}$pt$/1$ cup of mayonnaise. It can be doubled or tripled, but you will have trouble getting it to thicken if you try to halve it.

To make mayonnaise in a mixer: Put 2 egg yolks in a bowl, add $\frac{1}{4}$ teaspoon salt and $\frac{1}{4}$ teaspoon pepper and beat 30 seconds until slightly thickened. Add 1.75 dl$/6$ fl. oz$/\frac{3}{4}$ cup oil, drop by drop, beating constantly until the mixture starts to thicken. Once it starts to thicken, you can add the oil by teaspoonful or in a very slow stream, still beating constantly. When the mixture is very thick, add a tablespoon of vinegar, then continue beating in the remaining oil. Add more vinegar to taste. If the mayonnaise is oily, add more salt; if it tastes bland, add more pepper and a pinch of dry mustard, if you like.

To make mayonnaise in a blender: Follow the instructions for a mixer, adding the oil slightly more quickly so that the mayonnaise is less likely to curdle.

Braised Beef Roulades with Kidneys

4 thin slices of rump steak (about
   700 g/1½ lb)
225 g/½ lb ox kidney
2 shallots, chopped
2 tbs chopped parsley
salt and freshly ground black pepper
1 tbs oil
2 tbs butter
1 onion, diced
1 carrot, diced
2 stalks celery, diced
1 clove garlic, crushed
2 shallots, finely chopped
bouquet garni
1 tsp tomato paste
2.5 dl/½ pt/1 cup red wine
2.5 dl–3.25 dl/½–¾ pt/1–1½ cups stock
100 g/¼ lb mushrooms, thinly sliced
1 tbs chopped parsley (for sprinkling)

For kneaded butter
1½ tsp flour
1 tbs butter, softened

Quantities of this recipe can be halved,
doubled, or tripled. It reheats well.

Put the slices of steak between two sheets of
greaseproof paper and, with a cutlet bat or
a rolling pin, beat them out to ½ cm/¼ inch
thickness. Cut them in two crosswise. Cut
the core from the kidneys and dice them.
Spread kidneys on the steak, scatter with
the chopped shallots and parsley and
sprinkle with salt and pepper. Roll the
pieces of steak, tucking in the ends to make
neat bundles, and tie with string like par-
cels. Set the oven at moderately low (170°C,
Mark 3, 325°F).

In a heavy-based casserole, heat oil and
butter and fry the rolls on all sides over
medium heat until brown. Take out, add
the onion, carrot, and celery, lower the
heat, cover and cook 5–7 minutes until all
the fat is absorbed and the vegetables are
soft, but not brown. Add the garlic, shallots,
bouquet garni, tomato paste, wine, 1.25 dl/
¼ pt/1 cup stock, and seasoning, and
replace the beef rolls. Cover tightly, bring to
the boil and cook in the heated oven for 1¼–
1½ hours or until the rolls are very tender.
Add more stock during cooking if the pan
looks dry. Lift out the rolls, discard the
strings, and strain the cooking liquid. If
serving at once, reheat rolls briefly in the
cooking liquid. *You can prepare 48 hours
ahead up to this point.* Replace the rolls in
the casserole and pour over the cooking
liquid; keep in the refrigerator.

A short time before serving, skim any fat
from the pan and reheat the rolls in a moderate oven (180°C, Mark 4, 350°F) for 20–25
minutes or on top of the stove until very
hot. Lift them out and arrange on a dish.
Add the sliced mushrooms and simmer 2
minutes.

To make kneaded butter: With a fork, work
the flour into the butter until smooth.
Whisk it into the hot liquid, a piece at a
time, and simmer until the sauce thickens.
Taste sauce for seasoning, spoon it over the
rolls, sprinkle with parsley and serve.

Baked Barley

50 g/2 oz/¼ cup butter
1 onion, chopped
275 g/10 oz/1¼ cups pearl barley
5 dl/1 pt/2 cups beef stock
salt and pepper

This recipe can easily be doubled or tripled.
It reheats well.

Set oven at moderate (180°C, Mark 4, 350°F).

In a casserole melt the butter and sauté
the onion until soft. Add the barley and
cook, stirring, until browned. Pour in half
the stock, add salt and pepper, cover and
bake in the heated oven for 30 minutes.
Add the remaining stock, cover, and continue cooking 30 minutes longer or until all
the stock is absorbed and the barley is
tender.

To reheat it: Bake the barley in a
moderate oven (180°C, Mark 4, 350°F) for
15–20 minutes or over low heat on top of
stove until it is very hot.

Danish Peasant in a Veil

1 kg/2 lb tart apples
½ tsp ground cinnamon
½ tsp ground allspice
¼ tsp ground cloves
50–100 g/2–4 oz/¼–½ cup dark brown sugar
100 g/¼ lb semisweet chocolate, grated
2.5 dl/½ pt/1 cup double cream, stiffly
   whipped.

You can double or triple this recipe. The
flavour of the apple mixture matures if you
make it several days ahead, but the
whipped cream should be added only a
short time before serving.

Quarter the apples, discarding the small
black eye at the opposite end from the stalk.
Leave the apples unpeeled. Put them in a
heavy-based pan with ½ cm/¼ inch of water;
cover tightly and simmer on top of the
stove or bake in a moderate oven (180°C,
Mark 4, 350°F) for 15–20 minutes or until
very soft. Work through a food mill or sieve
and put the apple purée back in the casserole with the cinnamon, allspice, cloves,
and sugar to taste – the amount needed
depends on the tartness of the apples.
Simmer the apple mixture, stirring, on top
of the stove, or continue baking it in the
heated oven until thick but still soft enough
to fall from the spoon. Let cool, spread in a
glass serving bowl, cover tightly and chill.
*You can prepare 48 hours ahead up to this
point.*

Not more than three hours before
serving, sprinkle the apple mixture with
grated chocolate and pile the whipped
cream on top. Chill thoroughly.

Patio Lunch

Cold Lemon Soup
Seafood Pie
Green Salad
Peaches in Honey
Almond Wafers

The Greeks love to use lemons in cooking, and this soup is a version of their avgolemono, a lemon soup thickened with egg yolks and served cold. (When made as a light lemon and egg sauce, it is often served in Greece on lamb or vegetables.) The ingredients are so few that the flavour of the soup depends almost entirely on the quality of the chicken stock you use, and it is well worth making your own from a left-over chicken carcass or some chicken necks and backs (see page 210). Otherwise, use tinned rather than powdered chicken bouillon.

Seafood pie is one of those invaluable dishes that cannot go wrong, provided you can make good pastry. The baked pie shell is filled with seafood in a rich cream and wine sauce. Use any combination of fish you fancy – lobster, shrimps, and scallops if expense is no object, or white fish fillets with a judicious addition of a small amount of shellfish if you want to economize. You can make the pie ahead and reheat it or it can be frozen.

In summer the choice of lettuce for salad is almost unlimited. Bibb lettuce, cos, curly endive, corn salad, and several more varieties may be available at the same time. The success of a salad depends on texture as well as taste, so consider adding to the above, crisp and chewy watercress, spinach, and smooth, soft avocado. When choosing lettuce for salad, keep an eye on freshness and quality.

Honey, a traditional sweetener, has recently been rediscovered, thanks to the interest in health and natural foods. It has infinitely more taste than sugar, the flavours depending on which flower, tree, or shrub has attracted the bee; but whatever honey you choose, it will make an excellent, slightly tart syrup for poaching fruits like peaches. If you can find them, buy white instead of the more common yellow peaches. White peaches look smaller and less attractive, but their flavour is much superior. When peaches are out of season, the same honey syrup can be used for poaching whole pears or halved, cored apples. Light wafer biscuits, sprinkled with crisply browned almonds, are the ideal accompaniment.

COUNTDOWN

Day Before
Make lemon soup.
Make seafood pie.
Wash salad greens and keep in plastic
  bag; make dressing.
Poach peaches in honey and keep tightly
  covered.
Bake almond wafers and keep in airtight
  container.

45 Minutes Before Serving
Set oven at moderate (180°C, Mark 4,
  350°F).

30 Minutes Before Serving
Put pie in oven to reheat.

15 Minutes Before Serving
Chop chives, spoon soup into bowls, and
  add chives.
Put almond wafers on a plate.
Turn oven to low to keep pie warm.

After Serving Soup
Toss salad.

Cold Lemon Soup

pared rind and juice of 2 lemons
1 1/2 pt/4 cups well-flavoured chicken stock
  (page 210)
2 tbs rice
1.25 dl/$\frac{1}{4}$ pt/$\frac{1}{2}$ cup double cream
salt and pepper
1 tbs chopped chives

You can easily increase or halve the quantities of this soup.

Simmer the lemon rind and half the lemon
juice with the chicken stock and rice for 20
minutes or until the rice is very soft. Discard the lemon rind and work the soup
through a strainer to purée the rice. Chill
the soup, taste it, and add as much of the
remaining lemon juice as you like; *the acidity of lemons varies enormously and all the
juice may not be needed.* Whisk in the cream
– the soup will thicken slightly. *You can
prepare 24 hours ahead up to this point.*
   Taste the soup for seasoning and sprinkle
a few chives on each bowl before serving.

Seafood Pie

2.5 dl/½ pt/1 cup white wine
100 g/¼ lb scallops
100 g/¼ lb brill or other white fish fillets, cut
   in ½ cm/1-inch strips
100 g/¼ lb cooked peeled medium shrimps
100 g/¼ lb cooked lobster meat or crab meat
23–25 cm/9–10 inch baked flan or deep pie
   shell (see next recipe)
2½ tbs butter
2½ tbs flour
1.25 dl/¼ pt/½ cup milk
salt and pepper
pinch grated nutmeg
2 tbs sherry
2 egg yolks (optional)
1.25 dl/¼ pt/½ cup cream
50 g/2 oz/½ cup grated Gruyère or
   Parmesan cheese

If you are doubling or tripling this recipe, it is easiest to make two or three small pies rather than one large one.

Boil the wine until reduced by half. Cut large scallops in thick slices or leave small scallops whole. Add scallops to the wine, bring almost to the boil, and let stand off the heat for 1 minute. *Do not overcook scallops or they will be rubbery.* Lift out scallops with a slotted spoon and reserve them. Add the white fish strips to the pan, bring just to the boil, and let stand also for 1 minute. Lift out with a slotted spoon and add to scallops; reserve cooking liquid. Spread the fish and scallops in the baked pie shell with the shrimps and lobster or crab meat.

In a saucepan melt the butter, stir in the flour, and, when it is foaming, pour in the milk, the reserved cooking liquid, salt, pepper, and nutmeg. Bring to the boil, stirring constantly, and simmer 2 minutes. Add the sherry. Mix the egg yolks with the cream, stir in a little of the hot sauce, and stir this mixture back into the remaining sauce. Reheat the sauce gently until it thickens slightly – *do not boil or it will curdle.* If the pie is to be frozen, omit the egg yolks and add the cream directly to the sauce. Taste the sauce for seasoning and spoon it over the seafood in the pie shell. Sprinkle the top with grated cheese. *You can prepare 24 hours ahead up to this point.*

To serve: Set the oven at moderate (180°C, Mark 4, 350°F). Cook the pie in the heated oven until it is very hot and browned, allowing 15–20 minutes if it was freshly prepared or 25–30 minutes if it needed reheating.

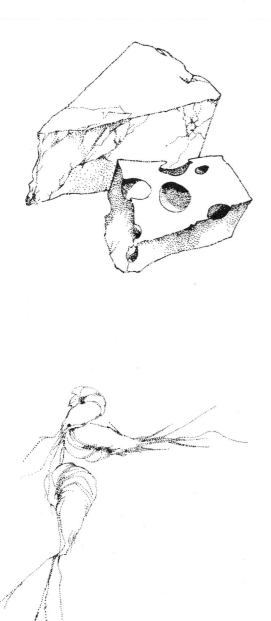

Pie Pastry Shell

225 g/½ lb/1½ cups flour
½ tsp salt
50 g/2 oz/¼ cup butter
50 g/2 oz/¼ cup cooking fat
2–3 tbs cold water

23–26 cm/9–10 inch flan ring or pie tin

To make the dough: Sift the flour into a bowl
with the salt. Add the butter and fat, and
cut it into small pieces with two knives.
Rub the fat into the flour with your fingertips until the mixture resembles crumbs.
Add 2 tablespoons water and mix with a
knife, Knead lightly with your hand, adding
more water if necessary to make a smooth
dough. Chill 30 minutes.

Roll out the dough and line it into the
flan ring or pie tin, pressing it well into the
corners with a ball of dough dipped in flour.
Chill it 30 minutes or until firm.

To bake an empty pie shell: Set the oven at
moderately hot (190°C, Mark 5, 375°F). Line
the pie shell with greaseproof paper, pressing it into the corners, and fill it with dried
beans or rice; this helps the dough keep its
shape during baking. Bake in the heated
oven for 15 minutes or until the pastry
starts to brown. Lift out the greaseproof
paper and beans and continue baking the
shell 8–10 minutes or until golden brown. If
using a flan ring, transfer the shell to a
rack to cool; if using a pie tin, let the shell
cool in the tin.

Green Salad

The ingredients for green salad are a matter of the season and your personal choice. Anything green can go in it – Bibb, cos, iceberg, or any of the other many kinds of lettuce; watercress; endive; escarole; chicory; spinach; or even a few slices of avocado. Try to make a contrast of crisp and tender, bland and sharp ingredients – for example, endive is excellent with watercress, and a few leaves of spinach will pep up cabbage lettuce. The only prohibitions are strong vegetables like cabbage and celery, whose flavour and texture are too overpowering, and coloured vegetables like tomatoes, which spoil the general aesthetic effect.

The vinaigrette dressing for green salad also depends on your personal taste. On the whole, delicate oil and a light vinegar go best with lettuce, but endive and chicory benefit from heavier oil and a touch of mustard; the flavour of watercress is developed when lemon juice is used instead of vinegar. Many people like a suspicion of garlic and some insist on a few finely chopped spring onions. Fresh herbs like chives, tarragon, basil, and oregano are a perfect addition when you can find them, but the dried versions do not have the same fragrance and are best omitted.

Salad vegetables should be carefully washed, torn (not cut) into bite-sized pieces, and dried thoroughly on a cloth or in a salad basket so that no water is left to dilute the dressing. Many greens benefit from being chilled an hour or two so they become crisp. About 450 g/1 pound will serve four people, and they will need about 1.25 dl/$\frac{1}{4}$ pt/$\frac{1}{2}$ cup of dressing (page 41). Dressing should be added to the salad at the last minute, then tossed well – the French call this *fatiguer* or to tire the salad and it is an apt description since the leaves wilt slightly as they absorb the dressing. Serve the salad at once because the leaves soften rapidly and will be unpleasantly soggy after an hour or two.

Peaches in Honey

350 g/¾ lb/1 cup honey
7.5 dl/1½ pt/3 cups water
1 vanilla pod or 1 tsp vanilla extract
5–6 large ripe peaches
squeeze lemon juice

Vanilla pod comes from a type of orchid, and is much more perfumed than vanilla extract; it should be split to release the seeds during cooking. Most good grocers sell vanilla pods; they are expensive, but they can be rinsed after use and dried to use again. If you double this recipe, poach the peaches in several batches, so they are always covered with syrup during poaching. You can prepare them a day or two ahead.

In a small deep saucepan heat the honey with the water and vanilla pod until dissolved. Do not add vanilla extract at this point. Add half the peaches – *they should all be completely covered with syrup*. If necessary add a little extra water. Cook over very low heat so the syrup just bubbles for 10–15 minutes or until the peaches are just tender. Lift them out with a slotted spoon, let cool slightly, and peel off the skin – the red part of the skin will have left a pretty pink blush on the flesh. Cook the remaining peaches in the same way, peel them, and arrange them in a shallow glass bowl. Boil the honey mixture until it is syrupy, let cool slightly, add a squeeze of lemon juice and vanilla extract, if used, and pour over the peaches; remove the vanilla pod. Cover tightly and chill.

Almond Wafers

100 g/¼ lb/¾ cup flour
pinch of salt
100 g/¼ lb/½ cup butter
100 g/¼ lb/½ cup sugar
3 egg whites
¼ tsp almond extract
50 g/2 oz/½ cup sliced almonds

This recipe can be doubled, and the wafers keep well in an airtight container. Makes about 30 wafers.

Set the oven at hot (200°C, Mark 6, 400°F) and grease and flour 2 baking sheets.

Sift the flour with salt. Cream the butter, gradually beat in the sugar, and continue beating until soft and light. Beat in the egg whites one by one, beating well after each addition. Beat in 1 tablespoon of the measured flour after each egg white. Fold in the remaining flour and stir in the almond extract and almonds as lightly as possible.

Drop teaspoonful of the mixture on the prepared baking sheet, leaving plenty of space for it to spread, and bake in the heated oven for 6–7 minutes until the edges of the wafers are golden. Transfer to a rack to cool.

Last-Minute Supper

Caesar Salad

Veal Scaloppine with Mushrooms

Buttered Noodles

Zabaglione

Italian cooking has contributed most, but not all, of this menu. You can be excused for thinking Caesar salad comes from Rome, but in fact it is American. Since its creation in the 1920's by Caesar Cardini in Tijuana, Mexico, just over the California border, it has been adopted by innumerable chefs throughout the world. There are almost as many versions of the salad as there are chefs, but most agree that cos is the right kind of lettuce and that the dressing should include anchovy, lemon juice, Parmesan cheese, and a raw or lightly coddled egg. Like all green salads, it must be mixed at the last minute. Some people say not to cut the lettuce but leave it whole to eat it with the fingers leaf by leaf.

The rest of the menu – veal scaloppine and zabaglione – is truly Italian. The scaloppine, tiny thin slices of veal which are sautéed in butter with mushrooms before being simmered in white wine, are an Italian favourite – and no wonder, when their veal is so good. Similar milk-fed veal is usually only available from very high quality butchers and is instantly recognizable by its pale pink colour untinged by red or grey, and when fresh it is shiny, with no trace of dryness at the edges. It is expensive, but you will need relatively little since 675 g or $1\frac{1}{2}$ lb will amply serve you and three guests.

In restaurants, zabaglione often costs more than the standard desserts. You are paying for the five minutes of labour, not the ingredients of egg yolks, sugar, and Marsala, the sweet dark wine from Sicily. Zabaglione is at its best whipped up on the stove and served while still warm, though you can make it up to an hour ahead if it is whisked until cool before being poured into stemmed glasses. As with soufflés and other feathery concoctions, the idea is to lighten the mixture with the maximum amount of air. For this it is best to use a balloon whisk and a copper bowl (page 208), set over a pan of simmering water. Be careful not to let the zabaglione cook too quickly or get too hot or it will curdle.

COUNTDOWN

1 Hour Before Serving
Wash lettuce; fry croûtons; assemble
  ingredients for Caesar salad.

40 Minutes Before Serving
Cook veal, but do not add cream.

20 Minutes Before Serving
If making zabaglione ahead, start beating
  egg mixture.

15 Minutes Before Serving
Start cooking noodles.
Finish zabaglione and chill.

5 Minutes Before Serving
Drain noodles and leave in fresh warm
  water.
Toss salad in the kitchen or at the table.

After Serving Salad
Reheat veal and add cream.
Drain noodles and toss in butter.

After Serving Veal
Make zabaglione if not already prepared.

Caesar Salad

1 head cos lettuce, washed
1.25 dl/$\frac{1}{4}$ pt/$\frac{1}{2}$ cup olive oil
2 garlic cloves, bruised
2 slices stale French bread or 1 crusty roll,
  diced (for croûtons)
4 anchovy fillets, chopped
juice $\frac{1}{2}$ lemon
salt and freshly ground black pepper
1 egg
2 tbs grated Parmesan cheese

You can halve, double, or triple this salad.

Tear lettuce into bite-sized pieces, put in a
salad bowl, and chill. To make croûtons:
Heat 3 tablespoons of the olive oil with
garlic cloves; add diced bread and fry, stirring until evenly browned. Drain croûtons
on paper towels, discarding garlic.

   Just before serving, add remaining olive
oil to lettuce and toss well. Add anchovy,
lemon juice, salt and pepper, and toss
again. Break in the egg and toss until leaves
are well coated. Lastly add cheese and
croûtons, toss again and taste for seasoning,
adding more salt, pepper, or lemon juice if
necessary.

Veal Scaloppine with Mushrooms

675 g/1½ lb veal scaloppine, cut in
   5–8 cm/2–3-inch squares
25 g/1 oz/¼ cup flour mixed with ½ tsp salt
   and ¼ tsp pepper.
50 g/2 oz/¼ cup butter
225 g/½ lb mushrooms, thinly sliced
2.5 dl/½ pt/1 cup white wine
2.5 dl/½ pt/1 cup double cream
1 tbs chopped parsley (for garnish)

This recipe can be halved or doubled, and it
reheats well.

Coat the veal with the seasoned flour. In a
large pan melt half the butter and brown
half the pieces of veal on both sides over
medium heat. Take them out, add the
remaining butter and brown the remaining
pieces of veal. Put all the veal in the pan,
add the mushrooms, and pour over the
wine. Cover and simmer 10–15 minutes
until the veal is very tender. *You can prepare
ahead up to this point.*

   Reheat the veal, add the cream and bring
just back to the boil. Taste for seasoning,
transfer to a serving dish and sprinkle with
parsley.

Buttered Noodles

350 g/¾ lb noodles
salt and freshly ground black pepper
100 g/¼ lb/¼ cup butter

Don't try to cook more than double quantity of noodles unless you have a very large
pan because they tend to stick together
during cooking.

Simmer the noodles in a large pan of salted
water for 10–12 minutes or until almost
tender but still firm to the teeth (*al dente*).
Drain and rinse with warm water to wash
away the starch. Melt the butter in the pan,
add the noodles with plenty of pepper and
toss over the heat until very hot. Serve at
once.

   To keep noodles hot for up to ½ hour:
Cook, drain, and rinse them. Return them
to the pan with a 5 cm/2-inch covering of
warm water. Just before serving, drain,
rinse, and toss them in butter.

Zabaglione

6 egg yolks
6 tbs sugar
2.5 dl/$\frac{1}{2}$ pt/1 cup sweet Marsala
cats' tongues biscuits (for serving)

This recipe can be halved or made in as large a quantity as you can beat. Each egg yolk can absorb 1 tablespoon sugar and about 3 tablespoons Marsala. Use a large bowl if you double it, so the mixture is easy to whisk.

Put all the egg yolks, sugar, and Marsala in a bowl, preferably metal, over a pan of simmering water and heat, beating constantly until the mixture is light and thickens enough to leave a ribbon trail when the beater is lifted. *Do not allow the mixture to boil or it will curdle.* Take from the heat and continue beating 1 minute. If serving at once, pour into stemmed glasses. If preparing ahead, set the bowl in ice water and continue beating until the zabaglione is cold. Spoon into stemmed glasses and keep in the refrigerator for up to an hour before serving. Serve with cats' tongues biscuits.

MENUS
FOR SIX

Dinner Outdoors

A Quick Supper

A Summer Lunch

A Winter Lunch

MENUS FOR SIX

Cooking for six offers endless possibilities. With four or five guests, you can create whatever party you please – lunch, brunch, formal dinner, or a help-yourself buffet. This is the time for such personal touches as fresh flowers or an unusual table decoration. You will have no trouble serving such a small group yourself, so there is no need to hire professional help unless you want a formal atmosphere.

Simple food and hearty flavours best suit a Dinner Outdoors, and what could be more spectacular than a whole sea bass baked on a bed of tomatoes, mushrooms, and courgettes. A well-seasoned ham mousse, served with hot herb bread, can act both as an appetizer or the accompaniment to a pre-dinner bottle of wine – this is one occasion when a chilled rosé would be ideal.

For a more formal meal indoors, borrow the leg of lamb recipe in the Dinner for All Seasons under Menus for Eight. Simply buy a smaller leg of lamb and reduce the quantities of the accompaniments (but not the green peppercorn sauce). The mushroom and onion appetizer is easy to cut down in quantity, and although you may have some coffee charlotte dessert left over, it keeps well.

A Quick Supper needs to be ready at a few minutes' notice. Tomatoes stuffed with avocado purée take no time to prepare, so you can sit down and enjoy the appetizer while the entrée of scallops with herbs is baking in the oven. The remaining dishes in the menu – saffron rice and strawberries Romanoff – can both be prepared ahead.

Easily adaptable for six is the Fireside Dinner suggested in Menus for Two, though you will have to spend rather more time on preparation. But steak stuffed with mushrooms, followed by a wine-laden dessert of whipped cream, is surely worth the extra effort.

Winter and summer alike, a leisurely lunch is a rare treat. A Summer Lunch includes chicken crêpes, rich with cream sauce and gilded with cheese, and raspberries, one of the season's most glorious fruits, made into a summer pudding. With a flavour all its own, this much neglected dessert – made only with raspberries, sugar, and dry bread – adds up to much more than the sum of its simple in-gredients. This menu is also ideal for brunch.

A Winter Lunch needs to satisfy rather than stimulate the appetite. Try steaming hot artichokes, stuffed with ham, followed by pojarski, which are minced veal cutlets in a brandy-laced mushroom sauce. The dessert of pavlova, a frosty crisp meringue, filled with fresh pineapple and cream, will compete for attention with any snowscape outside.

Dinner Outdoors

Ham Mousse
Hot Herb French Bread
Baked Fish St Aubin
Figs with Walnut Bread

This menu has the feeling of southern France, although strictly speaking, none of the recipes are Provençal. But you might be served similar uncomplicated cooking on the terrace of a country inn anywhere in the Midi.

A well-flavoured ham, rich and creamy but piquant, makes excellent mousse. In this recipe, the mousse is presented in a bowl or soufflé dish, but to dress it up, you can glaze the surface with aspic, add a decorative design of sliced cucumbers and hard-boiled eggs (and even truffles if you are feeling extravagant) before sealing it with another layer of aspic. In place of the hot herb loaf suggested here, you can serve the mousse with whole wheat bread or simply with good crackers.

As mentioned, a big, colourful baked fish is the centrepiece. The fish is cooked on a bed of mushrooms, tomatoes, and courgettes and, after absorbing their flavours, comes to the table garnished with these vegetables. The kind of fish – bass, grey mullet, bream or John Dorey are all delicious – does not matter nearly as much as its freshness. Since white fish lose flavour after even a day or two of refrigeration, try to find them freshly caught. The telltale signs are bright eyes, firm shiny flesh, and bright red gills.

In climates where fig trees flourish, people often combine cheese with figs for dessert. In this recipe, they are set on rounds of walnut bread, flavoured with maple syrup or honey and made crunchy with nuts. Fresh figs are, of course, the best, but tinned ones can be substituted; dried figs will not do in this recipe.

COUNTDOWN

Several Days Ahead
Make walnut bread and keep in an airtight container.
Make ham mousse and keep tightly
covered.

In the Morning
Prepare herb bread and wrap in foil.
Make cream cheese mixture for figs.

1–2 Hours Before Serving
Prepare fish and keep covered.
Complete figs with cream cheese and
keep at room temperature.

1½ Hours Before Serving
Set oven at moderate (180°C, Mark 4,
350°F).

1–1¼ Hours Before Serving
Start baking large fish.

Or 30–40 Minutes Before Serving
Start baking two smaller fish.

15 Minutes Before Serving
Bake herb bread.

Just Before Serving
Turn oven to low to keep fish warm.

After Serving Mousse
Transfer fish and vegetables to a platter.

Ham Mousse

225 g/½ lb lean cooked ham, diced
1 tin 275 g/10½ oz consommé
2 tbs Madeira
½ tsp ground allspice
¼ tsp ground nutmeg
salt and freshly ground black pepper
2.5 dl/½ pt/1 cup double cream, stiffly
    whipped

serving bowl or soufflé dish (1 1/2 pt capacity)

Ham mousse improves if you make it a day
or two – or up to 5 days – ahead, but do
not try to freeze it. You can easily double or
triple this recipe.

Purée half the ham with half the consommé
in a blender. Take it out and purée the
remaining ham and consommé. Put the
mixture in a bowl and beat in the Madeira,
allspice, nutmeg, plenty of pepper, and salt,
if necessary – *if the ham is salty, extra salt
may not be needed.* Stir in a little of the
whipped cream to soften the mixture, then
fold in the rest lightly. Pile into a serving
bowl or soufflé dish, cover and chill.

Hot Herb French Bread

1 loaf French bread
225 g/½ lb butter
1 tbs chopped parsley
2 tsp chopped chives
1 tsp tarragon

It is easy to make more or less of this bread.

Cut the loaf in diagonal 4–5 cm/1½–2-inch slices, almost but not quite to the bottom of the loaf. Melt the butter in a pan with the parsley, chives, and tarragon. Force the slices of bread slightly apart and brush them generously with herb butter. Brush any remaining butter on top of the loaf and wrap it in foil.

A short time before serving, bake it in a moderate oven (180°C, Mark 4, 350°F) for 10 minutes, open foil and bake 5 minutes more or until crisp.

Baked Fish St Aubin

100 g/¼ lb/½ cup butter, softened
350 g/¾ lb mushrooms, thinly sliced
700 g/1½ lb courgettes, cut in 1 cm/¼ inch
    slices
6 large tomatoes, peeled and sliced
    (page 207)
salt and freshly ground black pepper
2½–3 kg/6–7 lb whole fish – sea bass, grey
    mullet, bream or John Dorey – or 2
    smaller fish of 1½–2 kg/3½–4 lb each,
    cleaned with head left on
1 tsp thyme
1 tsp basil
1 tsp oregano

You can make this recipe in larger or smaller quantities – allow about 450 g/1 lb of fish per person, including head and bones. Baking time is about 10 minutes per pound.

Butter a large baking dish or roasting pan, spread the mushrooms and courgettes in the bottom, and top with the tomatoes. Sprinkle with salt and pepper. Wash the fish, pat dry with paper towels, and score the flesh deeply with 4 or 5 diagonal slashes. Spread the butter on the fish, set it on top of the vegetables and sprinkle with the thyme, basil, oregano, and plenty of salt and pepper. *You can prepare 2–3 hours ahead up to this point.*

Bake the fish in a moderate oven (180°C, Mark 4, 350°F), allowing 1–1¼ hours for the large fish or 30–40 minutes for the smaller ones or until the flesh flakes easily. Transfer the fish to a long platter, spoon the vegetables beside it and serve at once.

Figs with Walnut Bread

1 package 225 g/8 oz cream cheese
1–2 tbs sugar (or to taste)
3–4 tbs single cream
12–14 fresh figs (about 350 g/$\frac{3}{4}$ lb) or 2 tins
    (475 g/17 oz each) figs, drained

For walnut bread
225 g/$\frac{1}{2}$ lb/2 cups flour
125 g/$\frac{1}{4}$ lb/$\frac{1}{2}$ cup sugar
1.25 dl/$\frac{1}{4}$ pt/$\frac{1}{2}$ cup maple syrup or honey
1.8 dl/6 fl.oz/$\frac{3}{4}$ cup milk
pinch of salt
3 tsp baking powder
1 egg, beaten to mix
75 g/3 oz/$\frac{3}{4}$ cup coarsely chopped walnuts

two 500 g/18 oz tins, tops discarded

Empty tins make baking pans of ideal size
for this walnut bread.

For the walnut bread: Set the oven at moderate (180°C, Mark 4, 350°F). Grease the tins, line the bases with a circle of greaseproof paper, and grease again. Sprinkle them with flour, discarding the excess.

Gently heat the sugar, maple syrup or honey, and milk, stirring constantly, until the sugar dissolves. Let cool. Sift the flour, salt, and baking powder together into a bowl and make a well in the centre. Stir the cooled sugar mixture into the egg and pour into the well in the flour. Stir until smooth, then stir in the walnuts, and spoon the batter into the prepared tins. Bake in the heated oven for 1 hour and 15 minutes or until a skewer inserted in the centre comes out clean. Let cool slightly, then turn out on a wire rack to cool completely. The breads can be kept for up to a week in an airtight container.

An hour or two before serving, work the cream cheese until soft and beat in sugar to taste and enough cream to make a mixture that just falls from the spoon. Cut the walnut bread into rounds 2 cm/$\frac{3}{4}$ inch thick, discarding the round tops. Spread each round with the cream cheese mixture and set a fig in the centre; arrange on a platter for serving.

A Quick Supper

Tomatoes Stuffed with Guacamole

Baked Scallops with Herb Butter

Saffron Rice

stems from the new varieties which are bred more for symmetry and solidity than for taste. Part is the practice of gathering tomatoes while still green and letting them ripen after picking to avoid waste. The results are plain for all to see – pallid tomatoes with a greenish tinge that look and taste quite different from the plump glowing red of vine-ripened fruit. Locally

tomatoes are available for part of the so seek them out.

hing could be simpler than scallops with butter and herbs. If you can, nd serve them in little individual es, or baking dishes, so that all the r and aroma are retained in the cook- d the guests can savour the smell the lids are lifted at the table.

version of pilaf becomes a cheerful colour when baked in the oven with . Saffron is made from the dried s of the autumn crocus and every must be picked by hand; this makes most expensive spice. But luckily a of saffron is sufficient to season most . It gives a characteristic flavour to and bouillabaisse.

wberries Romanoff is one of the many dishes that were created in Russia in yday of the czars, when French chefs anded handsome salaries at the royal This light but rich dessert is made of whipped cream flavoured with orange juice, orange liqueur, and crushed strawberries. If your market's strawberries smell fragrant, you can be fairly sure that they are good, but the most reliable test, of course, is to taste them.

Walnut Bread

COUNTDOWN

Day Before
Cook the rice.
Make strawberries Romanoff and keep
    tightly covered.

In the Morning
Prepare avocado mixture and tomatoes,
    but do not fill.
Prepare scallops for baking.

15 Minutes Before Serving
Set oven at hot (220°C, Mark 7, 425°F).
Reheat rice over low heat on top of
    stove.
Fill tomatoes.

While Serving Appetizer
Keep rice in a warm place.
Bake scallops.

Tomatoes Stuffed with Guacamole

6 large vine-ripened tomatoes, peeled
    (page 207)
2 ripe avocados
2 tbs lime or lemon juice
1 small tinned chili, drained and chopped
1 tbs finely chopped onion
salt and freshly ground black pepper

If you don't want to open a tin of chilis,
you can substitute 1–2 teaspoons chili
powder. The recipe can be halved or
doubled.

Discard the core of the tomatoes, turn them
over, and cut off the tops to make lids,
scooping out the seeds with a teaspoon.
Strain the seeds and reserve the juice. Halve
the avocados, peel them, and on a plate add
the reserved tomato juice, lime or lemon
juice, chili, onion, and plenty of salt and
pepper. Mash with a fork to a purée and
taste for seasoning. Cover tightly and chill
avocado mixture and tomatoes, *You can prepare ahead up to this point.*
  A short time before serving, fill the
tomatoes with the avocado mixture; set the
lids on top at a slant and serve.

Baked Scallops with Herb Butter

$1\frac{3}{4}$ kg/$2\frac{1}{2}$ lb scallops
175 g/6 oz/$\frac{3}{4}$ cup butter
3 shallots, finely chopped
1 clove garlic, crushed (optional)
2 tbs chopped parsley
1 tbs chopped chives
2 tsp chopped fresh tarragon or basil
salt and freshly ground black pepper

*6 individual cocottes, or baking dishes with
lids, or 1 shallow baking dish (2 1/4 pt/2-quart
capacity) with lid.*

You can easily double or halve the recipe. If
you cannot find fresh tarragon or basil, use
half quantity of the dried herb.

Discard the small white membrane adhering
to the side of the scallops, drain them, and
divide them among 6 cocottes, or individual
baking dishes with lids, or 1 shallow baking
dish. Melt the butter, stir in the shallots,
garlic if used, parsley, chives, tarragon or
basil, salt and pepper. Spoon the mixture
over the scallops and cover with the lids.
*You can prepare 3–4 hours ahead up to this
point.*

A short time before serving, bake the
scallops in a hot oven (220°C, Mark 7,
425°F), allowing 10 minutes for the individual dishes or 15–20 minutes for the large
one, or until the scallops are no longer
transparent in the centre. *Do not overcook
them or they will be rubbery.* Serve at once in
the baking dishes. Leave guests to remove
the lids on individual dishes.

Saffron Rice

3 tbs butter
1 onion, chopped
350 g/$\frac{3}{4}$ lb/$1\frac{1}{2}$ cups rice
pinch of saffron, soaked for 15 minutes in
    4 tbs hot water.
6.25 dl/$1\frac{1}{4}$ pt/$2\frac{3}{4}$ cups water
salt and pepper

This recipe can easily be doubled or tripled,
and it reheats well.

In a casserole melt the butter and sauté the
onion until soft but not brown. Add the rice
and cook, stirring for 1–2 minutes until the
grains are transparent. Add the saffron and
water, salt and pepper, cover and bring to
the boil. Simmer on top of the stove or cook
in a moderate oven (180°C, Mark 4, 350°F)
for exactly 20 minutes. Let the rice cool 10
minutes before stirring it with a fork to fluff
up the grains.

To reheat: Put rice, covered, in a moderate oven (180°C, Mark 4, 350°F) for 15–20
minutes or heat it gently on top of the stove
until very hot.

Strawberries Romanoff

1.5 kg/3 lb fresh strawberries
grated rind and juice 1 orange
4 tbs Grand Marnier, Curaçao, or other
    orange liqueur
2 tbs brandy
4–6 tbs sugar
3.25 dl/¾ pt/1½ cups double cream, stiffly
    whipped

You can double or triple this recipe or make
half quantity; the flavour mellows if it is
prepared 12–24 hours in advance.

Hull the strawberries and wash them only if
they are very sandy. Crush them with a
fork, add the orange rind and juice, orange
liqueur, brandy, and sugar to taste (the
amount needed depends on the sweetness of
the strawberries) and stir until the sugar is
dissolved. Stir this mixture into the whipped
cream and pile it in a glass bowl. Cover it
tightly and chill at least 6 hours or up to 24
hours.

A Summer Lunch

Chicken Crêpes
Green Bean and Walnut Salad
Raspberry Summer Pudding

Chicken crêpes have everything a cook could ask for. Their rich creamy sauce has universal appeal, they can be prepared days or even weeks ahead, and they are easy to make for six, sixteen, or sixty people. Added to the bargain, chicken crêpes are relatively inexpensive. With them, the crunchy texture of green bean and walnut salad is an excellent contrast.

The perfect lacy-thin crêpe requires a little practice to make, but once you have mastered the knack, they are quick and easy. If you don't have the special shallow 15 cm / 6-inch crêpe pan, any well-seasoned frying pan will do; an omelette pan is ideal. The batter must be the consistency of thin cream. You will need only a very little oil for frying – one coating of oil in the pan should be enough to fry about 6 crêpes and the first one will probably be a failure because the pan was too greasy. When you add the batter, the knack is to quickly tip the pan to every side so that the base is evenly coated. Crêpes should be cooked quickly – about 25 seconds for the first side, 10 for the second. Some professionals flip them; others turn with a spatula, so either way you are in good company.

Crêpes are extraordinarily versatile. They can be filled with almost any creamy ingredients – the seafood pie mixture (page 50) is particularly good – or they can be used in desserts like crêpes Suzette. Some cooks add a tablespoon of sugar to the batter for sweet crêpes, but it is not really necessary.

Summer pudding is an old-fashioned dessert that tends to be passed over in modern cookbooks. Despite its humble origins, in an era when people preferred to eat old bread rather than throw it away, summer pudding has a distinguished flavour. It consists of poached tart fruits, such as raspberries, blackberries, or blackcurrants, moulded in a deep bowl with sliced dry bread. Weighted down for a day or two, the bread absorbs all the juices from the fruit, and the pudding which results turns out easily onto a dish.

COUNTDOWN

1–2 Days Before
Cook chicken, make crêpes and fill; cover
  tightly.
Make summer pudding.
Make vinaigrette dressing for salad.

In the Morning
Cook green beans, chop parsley.

45 Minutes Before Serving
Set oven at moderate (180°C, Mark 4,
  350°F).
Mix salad and leave at room
  temperature.
Turn out and decorate summer pudding.

30 Minutes Before Serving
Put crêpes in oven.

Just Before Serving
Add parsley to salad.

Chicken Crêpes

1¾–2 kg/4–4½ lb whole roasting chicken or
  fowl
1 onion, quartered
1 carrot, quartered
bouquet garni
6 peppercorns
salt
1.25 dl/¼ pt/½ cup oil (for frying)
75 g/3 oz/¼ cup grated Parmesan cheese (for
  sprinkling) – optional

For crêpe batter
100 g/¼ lb/1 cup flour
pinch of salt
1 egg
1 egg yolk
3.75 dl/¾ pt/1½ cups milk
2 tbs melted butter

For the filling
350 g/¾ lb mushrooms, sliced
juice ½ lemon
freshly ground black pepper
6 tbs butter
6 tbs flour
3.75 dl/¾ pt/1½ cups single cream

15–18 cm/6–7 inch diameter crêpe pan

This recipe makes about 18 crêpes; it can
easily be doubled or tripled.

To poach the chicken: Put the chicken with
the onion, carrot, bouquet garni, peppercorns, and a little salt in a pan with water
to cover. Cover and simmer 50–60 minutes
for a roasting chicken or 1¼–1½ hours for a
fowl or until the bird is very tender. Let cool
in the liquid, then take the meat from the
bones and divide it into small pieces, tearing

rather than cutting it. Reserve the meat.
Put the bones and skin back in the cooking
broth, cover and simmer 1–1½ hours to
extract the flavour from the bones. Strain
the stock and boil until reduced to
7.5 dl/1½ pt/3 cups. Chill and discard the fat
which solidifies on the surface.

To make the crêpes: Sift flour with salt into a
bowl, make a well in the centre and add the
egg and egg yolk. Slowly add half the milk,
stirring constantly to form a smooth batter.
Beat 2 minutes. Stir in the melted butter
with half the remaining milk, cover, and let
the batter stand 30 minutes. It will thicken
slightly as the grains of starch in the flour
expand. Stir in enough of the remaining
milk to make a batter the consistency of
thin cream.

   Heat the oil in the crêpe pan until very
hot (a drop of batter will sizzle at once).
Pour the oil into a heatproof cup and add
2–3 tablespoons batter to the pan, turning
the pan quickly so the bottom is
evenly coated. Cook over fairly high heat
until browned, then toss the crêpe or
turn with a spatula. Cook for 10 seconds to
brown the other side and turn out onto a
plate. Continue cooking the remaining
crêpes in the same way, re-oiling the pan
only when the crêpes start to stick. As they
are cooked, pile one on top of another to
keep the bottom ones moist and warm. You
can make the crêpes ahead; layer them
with greaseproof paper, put them in a
plastic bag, and keep them in the refrigerator for 2–3 days or up to 2 months in
the freezer.

To cook the mushrooms: Put them in a pan
with the lemon juice and a little pepper and
add 1 cm/½ inch of water. Cover and cook
over high heat for 2–3 minutes or until the
liquid bubbles to the top of the pan. Let cool
slightly, add the mushrooms to the chicken
and reserve the cooking liquid.

To make the sauce: In a pan, melt the butter,
stir in the flour, and, when foaming, add
the reserved chicken stock and liquid from
cooking the mushrooms.
Bring to the boil, stirring, and simmer 2
minutes. Add 2.5 dl/½ pt/1 cup cream,
bring just back to the boil and add salt and
pepper to taste. Add half this sauce to the
mushrooms and chicken and mix well.
   Put a tablespoonful of filling on each
crêpe, roll them like cigars, and arrange
them diagonally in one or two large buttered gratin dishes or shallow baking
dishes. Add the remaining 1.25 dl/¼ pt/½ cup
cream to the sauce, taste for seasoning, and
spoon the sauce over the crêpes to coat
them completely. Sprinkle the dish with
cheese. *You can prepare the crêpes ahead up to
this point.*
   To reheat them: Bake the crêpes in a
moderate oven (180°C, Mark 4, 350°F) for
25–30 minutes or until bubbling and
browned.

Green Bean and Walnut Salad

700 g/1½ lb green beans
100 g/¼ lb/1 cup walnut halves
1.25 dl/¼ pt/½ cup vinaigrette dressing
  (page 41)
2 tbs chopped parsley

You can easily increase or halve the quantities of this salad.

Cook and drain the beans (see page 86) and cut them in 5–8 cm/2–3-inch lengths. An hour or two before serving, mix the beans and walnuts with vinaigrette dressing and leave covered at room temperature. Just before serving, add the parsley, mix again and serve.

Raspberry Summer Pudding

15–16 slices white bread (about ¾ of a
  450 g/1 lb loaf)
3 packages frozen raspberries, thawed
100 g/¼ lb/½ cup sugar
1.25 dl/¼ pt/¾ cup double cream stiffly
  whipped (for decoration)

*deep bowl or soufflé dish (1 l/1¾ pt/7–8-cup
capacity); icing bag and medium star nozzle.*

You can double or triple this recipe, but mould it in two or three bowls, not one large one.

Leave the slices of bread in a warm place for several hours so the texture becomes firm. Remove the crusts from the bread. Drain the raspberries, reserving the juice. Heat the sugar with the juice until dissolved, bring to the boil and simmer 2 minutes. Add the raspberries to the syrup and cook 1 minute more.

Spoon a little syrup into the bowl, add a layer of bread, and continue to line the bowl or soufflé dish with syrup and bread, overlapping the slices and curving them up the sides. Use only ⅔ of the bread. Put half the raspberries in the lined bowl, cover with half the remaining bread, add the rest of the raspberries, and top with the remaining bread. Press the top layer down gently with the flat side of a spoon so the bread absorbs the syrup from the layer underneath. Cover the bowl with greaseproof paper and set a plate with a 1 kg/2 lb weight on top. Set the bowl on a plate to catch any drips and chill overnight or up to 36 hours.

A short time before serving, loosen the sides of the pudding with a small sharp knife. Turn it out onto a dish and pipe a ruff of whipped cream around the base, using an icing bag and star nozzle.

A Winter Lunch

*Artichokes Stuffed
with Ham
Pojarski
Braised Chicory
Pavlova*

This menu borrows from the cuisine of six nations. The artichokes are Italian, the pojarski are Russian in origin and French by adoption, chicory is Belgian, and pavlova, although named after the famous Russian ballerina, comes from Australia and New Zealand.

Artichokes stuffed with ham are an interesting alternative to the usual accompaniment of melted butter. Parboiled so that the hairy chokes can be scooped out to make a hollow for the stuffing, they are then baked in wine and stock. The cooking liquid makes a good dip for serving with the leaves and the stuffing is eaten with the bottom.

Pojarski are a superior kind of hamburger, indeed so superior that they are a speciality of Maxim's in Paris. They are said to have been named after a certain innkeeper in the town of Torzhok on the road between Leningrad and Moscow, but the recipe — minced veal or chicken beaten with cream, shaped into cutlets and fried – is typically French. The mushrooms and cream sauce is laced with brandy.

Chicory, welcome as a winter salad, is also excellent when baked to serve hot as a vegetable. Look for white, plump heads with little trace of green at the tip. Occasionally chicory can be bitter, but there is no way of detecting this until you taste it. Although it is expensive because it is usually imported, there is happily no waste to this vegetable.

Anna Pavlova is one of the few performing artists in this century to whom chefs have paid tribute. In the years following World War I, she took her dance company to Australia and New Zealand, and both countries lay claim to the dessert. The authentic version is filled with passion fruit or kiwi fruit. The base is a huge round of meringue, made slightly soft and crumbly by adding vinegar and cornflour, with whipped cream. You can add your choice of fruits as the filling – pineapple is particularly good.

COUNTDOWN

Several Days Ahead
Bake pavlova and store in an airtight
   container.

Day Before
Cook artichokes and keep covered.
Braise chicory and keep covered.
Prepare pineapple and keep in an airtight
   container.

In the Morning
Prepare pojarski cutlets.
Chop parsley for chicory.

1–2 Hours Before Serving
Whip cream and complete pavlova.

35 Minutes Before Serving
Set oven at moderate (180°C, Mark 4,
   350°F).

20 Minutes Before Serving
Put artichokes and chicory in oven to
   reheat.
Cook pojarski, turn oven to low, and
   keep pojarski warm; make sauce, but
   do not add to platter.

After Serving Artichokes
Coat pojarski with sauce; add chicory to
   platter and sprinkle with parsley.

Artichokes Stuffed with Ham

6 medium globe artichokes
3.25 dl/$\frac{3}{4}$ pt/$1\frac{1}{2}$ cups white wine
3.25 dl/$\frac{3}{4}$ pt/$1\frac{1}{2}$ cups stock

For the stuffing
3 shallots, chopped
100 g/$\frac{1}{4}$ lb/$\frac{1}{2}$ cup butter
350 g/$\frac{3}{4}$ lb/2 cups cooked chopped ham
100 g/$\frac{1}{4}$ lb/$1\frac{1}{2}$ cups fresh white breadcrumbs
2 cloves garlic, crushed
2 tbs chopped parsley
salt and freshly ground black pepper

The quantities of this recipe can be halved
or increased three or four times. If possible,
use well flavoured ham to enliven the
stuffing.

Cut tops and stems from artichokes and
trim spikes from remaining leaves with
scissors. Cook the artichokes in plenty of
boiling salted water for 20/30 minutes or
until a leaf can be pulled out with a sharp
tug. Drain them, and set upside-down on a
rack to drain until cold enough to handle.
Discard the inside leaves and scoop out the
hairy choke with a teaspoon, scraping the
bottom of the artichoke clean to form a
hollow cup. The artichokes are only partially cooked at this point so the hairy
choke will not scrape out as easily as usual.
   For the stuffing: Sauté the shallot in the
butter until soft but not brown and stir in
the ham, breadcrumbs, garlic, and parsley,
with plenty of pepper. Salt may not be
needed if ham is salty. Taste for seasoning
and spoon into the artichoke cavities.
   Set the artichokes in a deep casserole or
baking dish, pour over the wine and stock,
cover and cook in a moderate oven (180°C,

Pojarski

1 kg/2 lb minced veal
salt and freshly ground black pepper
2.5 dl/½ pt/1 cup double cream
little flour (for coating)
50 g/2 oz/¼ cup butter

For the sauce
250 g/½ lb mushrooms, finely sliced
squeeze of lemon juice
2 tbs water
4 tbs brandy
1.25 dl/¼ pt/½ cup white wine
2.5 dl/½ pt/1 cup double cream

Pojarski can be prepared ahead and reheated, but they are really at their best
when freshly cooked – they take only 10–15
minutes. The recipe can be doubled or
halved.

Work the veal through the fine plate of a
mincer once or twice until very finely
ground. Beat it with a wooden spoon or
with the dough hook of an electric mixer
for 3–4 minutes or until it leaves the sides
of the bowl in a ball. *This beating gives the
pojarskis a light, smooth texture.* Add plenty
of salt and pepper and beat in the cream, a
tablespoon at a time, beating well after each
addition. Divide the meat into 6–8 parts
and, working on a lightly floured board,
mould each into a cutlet shape about
2½ cm/1 inch thick. Put the mushrooms in
a buttered pan with the lemon juice, water,
and salt and pepper; cover with foil and the
lid and cook gently 3–4 minutes until
tender. *You can prepare 5–6 hours ahead up
to this point.* Keep the cutlets in the refrigerator.

A short time before serving, melt the
butter in a very large pan and sauté the
cutlets over medium heat for 4–5 minutes
on each side or until lightly browned. *Do
not brown too much.* Add the brandy to the
pan and flame. Arrange the cutlets, overlapping, down one side of a serving dish
and keep warm.

Add the wine to the pan and bring to the
boil, stirring to dissolve the pan juices.
Simmer 2 minutes, add the mushrooms
with their liquid and the cream. Bring just
to the boil and taste for seasoning. Spoon
the sauce over the cutlets. Arrange the
braised chicory on the other side of the
serving dish, sprinkle with chopped parsley,
and serve.

Mark 4, 350°F) for 35–40 minutes or until
the artichokes are very tender. Baste them
occasionally during cooking. *You can prepare
ahead up to this point.*

To reheat the artichokes: Cook them in a
moderate oven (180°C, Mark 4, 350°F) for
15–20 minutes or heat them gently on top
of the stove until very hot. Serve the artichokes in soup bowls, with the cooking
liquid spooned over them.

Braised Chicory

6–8 heads (about 1 kg/2 lb) chicory
50 g/2 oz/¼ cup butter
salt and pepper
1 tsp sugar
1 tbs chopped parsley (for sprinkling)

The best chicory is plump and firm, but if you can find only small thin ones, you will need two heads per person. You can cook almost any quantity of chicory by this method.

Set the oven at moderate (180°C, Mark 4, 350°F). Wipe the chicory, discard any wilted leaves, and trim the stems. With the point of a knife, hollow the stem so the chicory cooks more evenly. Thickly butter a casserole, lay the chicory in it, and sprinkle with salt, pepper, and the sugar. Cover and bake in the heated oven for 1 hour or until the chicory is very tender. Arrange it on a serving dish, sprinkle with parsley and serve.

Pavlova

225 g/½ lb/1 cup sugar
6 egg whites
1 tsp distilled white vinegar
1 tbs cornflour

For filling
1 medium pineapple
3–4 tbs sugar (optional)
2.5 dl/½ pt/1 cup double cream, stiffly
  whipped

non-stick silicone paper (optional)

You can halve this recipe; don't try to double it, but instead make two pavlovas.

Set the oven at very low (140°C, Mark 1, 275°F) and line a baking sheet with silicone paper or grease it and sprinkle generously with sugar.

Stiffly whip the egg whites. Beat in the sugar a tablespoon at a time; when all the sugar has been added, the meringue should

be stiff and glossy. Stir in the vinegar, sprinkle over the cornflour, and fold in as lightly as possible. Pile the mixture in a large round on the prepared baking sheet, hollow the centre slightly, and bake in the heated oven for 1½ hours or until the pavlova is very lightly browned and like marshmallow in the centre. *If it browns too quickly during cooking, reduce the oven temperature to 130°C, Mark 2, 250°F.* Let the pavlova cool to lukewarm, then carefully peel off the paper or lift it off the baking sheet and transfer to a wire rack to cool completely. *You can store pavlova up to a week in an airtight container.*

Not more than a day ahead, cut the peel from the pineapple, then core and slice it (see page 207). Cut it in chunks, and if it is very tart, sprinkle with a little sugar. A short time before serving pile half the whipped cream in the hollow of the pavlova, add the pineapple, and top with the remaining cream.

MENUS
FOR
EIGHT

Dinner for All Seasons

A Light Summer Buffet

A Sophisticated Supper

A Hearty Breakfast

MENUS FOR EIGHT

Eight is an ideal number for entertaining. There are sufficient guests to justify the special effort of a seated dinner
or few enough to make buffet service agreeably intimate.
Eight is not too many for the old-fashioned kind of breakfast where most dishes must be made at the last minute,
and eight is just right for the simple but sophisticated
supper at which the cook can forget the kitchen until 20
minutes before the meal.

The following Dinner for All Seasons with its unusual
braised leg of lamb is adaptable enough to serve all year for
lunch or dinner. Preparation is best begun a day ahead,
and with little to do at the last minute, the cook can turn
hostess when the party begins.

If there's no time for advance preparation, try the Dinner
in a Hurry in Menus for Ten. The quantities may seem
generous for eight people, but few guests will refuse seconds
of a sweet raspberry soufflé, and the soup and pork can be
reheated to serve later at a family meal.

The Light Summer Buffet is centred on two contrasting
cold chicken dishes – one with a light curry-flavoured
mayonnaise, the other in vinaigrette dressing with mushrooms cooked in wine. Alternatively if you want a warming
Winter Buffet, the cassoulet – meat and bean casserole –
from Menus for Ten is a hearty dish whose leftovers reheat
for family meals.

The Sophisticated Supper begins with the lightest cheese
soufflé imaginable, and its cooking time – 10–12 minutes –
is one of the reasons why the finishing touches for this
menu need take you no more than 20 minutes. The menu
would be good for a lunch party, too.

Bring back an old tradition – the Hearty Breakfast.
Skiers, hunters, and outdoor enthusiasts will welcome a
sustaining meal at the start of the day. Like most good

breakfasts, it cannot be made ahead, but the early morning effort is well worthwhile.

When a picnic strikes your fancy but only eight guests are invited, all you need do is omit one of the salad recipes from the Gourmet Picnic in Menus for Ten. The instant appeal of country terrine with homemade whole wheat bread will guarantee there is nothing left to carry back home.

Dinner for All Seasons

*Mushrooms and Onions à
la Grecque*

Braised Leg of Lamb

Green Peppercorn Sauce

Buttered Green Beans

Lima Bean Purée

*Coffee Charlotte with Cold
Chocolate Sauce*

This elegant menu is a useful stand-by because the dishes are equally good, winter and summer alike. The appetizer, mushrooms and onions à la Grecque, is a classic French salad, made pleasantly piquant with lemon and white wine. Several other vegetables – cauliflower, artichoke hearts, and courgettes – can be prepared in the same way, though cooking times must be adjusted. Charlotte refers to the bucket-shaped mould in which the dessert is set, and the word comes from the old English 'charlet' meaning custard. In their modern form, charlottes were introduced in the nineteenth century by the French chefs of the Russian court who gave them names like charlotte Malakoff and charlotte Russe.

A touch of the exotic is added to the main course by the green peppercorn sauce. This new spice from Madagascar is the familiar black peppercorn, gathered unripe and then pickled in vinegar. It has an intriguing freshness that blends well with rich flavours like salmon and duck as well as with beef and the braised lamb suggested here. Green peppercorns are available from certain food shops, but if you cannot find them, the lamb is still delicious served simply with the gravy made from the cooking liquid.

Most of the preparation for this menu can be done a day ahead, leaving only the vegetables to be cooked, the lamb to be reheated, and the charlotte to be decorated a short time before dinner. Even the green peppercorn sauce can be made an hour or two ahead, but it must then be reheated carefully in a bain-marie. The sauce is a version of the egg and butter sauce Béarnaise and, like Béarnaise, it curdles easily if overcooked.

COUNTDOWN

Day Before
Make mushrooms and onions à la
    Grecque and cover.
Braise leg of lamb and keep in casserole,
    ready for reheating.
Make lima bean purée and leave in pan
    ready for reheating.
Make coffee charlotte and cover.
Make chocolate sauce and keep covered.

In the Morning
Prepare green beans and keep in cold
    water.

1½–2 Hours Before Serving
Cook and drain green beans.
Unmould charlotte. Stiffly whip cream
    and decorate charlotte with rosettes;
    chill.
Make green peppercorn sauce and let
    cool.

1¼ Hours Before Serving
Set oven at moderately low (170°C, Mark
    3, 325°F).

1 Hour Before Serving
Put lamb in oven to reheat.

15 Minutes Before Serving
Reheat green peppercorn sauce in a bain-
    marie over very low heat; serve warm,
    not hot.
Reheat lima bean purée, pile in serving
    dish and keep warm.
Transfer lamb to serving dish and strain
    gravy.

After Serving Appetizer
Reheat green beans in butter.
Add watercress to lamb serving dish.

Mushrooms and Onions à la Grecque

700 g/1½ lb (about 24) tiny onions
2.5 dl/½ pt/1 cup white wine
2.5 dl/½ pt/1 cup stock
1 clove garlic, crushed
2 tsp tomato paste
juice ½ lemon
bouquet garni
salt (optional) and pepper
700 g/1½ lb small mushrooms
1 tbs chopped parsley
1 lemon, thinly sliced (for garnish)

This recipe can be halved, doubled, or
tripled with no problem. The flavour mellows if the dish is made at least a day
ahead.

Trim the mushroom stems level with the
caps. Blanch the onions in boiling water for
1 minute, drain and peel them – the skins
will strip away easily. Trim the roots and
stems of the onions carefully so they will
not fall apart during cooking.
    In a shallow pan combine the onions,
wine, stock, garlic, tomato paste, lemon
juice, bouquet garni, and a little pepper.
Bring to the boil and simmer, uncovered,
for 8–10 minutes or until the onions are
almost tender. Add the mushrooms and
simmer 2 minutes longer or until the mushrooms are cooked. Transfer the vegetables
to a serving dish. Boil the cooking liquid
until reduced to 2.5 dl/½ pt/1 cup and taste
for seasoning – it should be quite piquant,
Discard bouquet garni, pour the liquid over
the mushrooms and onions, cover and chill
for at least 1 and up to 4 days.
    Just before serving, sprinkle the veget-
ables with chopped parsley and arrange the
lemon slices on top.

Braised Leg of Lamb

3 tbs oil
2½–3 kg/6–7 lb leg of lamb
2 onions, diced
2 carrots, diced
bouquet garni
1 tsp rosemary
1 clove garlic, crushed
salt and pepper
5 dl/1 pt/2 cups white wine
2.5 dl/½ pt/1 cup beef stock
1 bunch watercress (for garnish)
green peppercorn sauce (for serving)

To make this recipe for fewer people, use a smaller leg of lamb, but keep the remaining ingredients the same. If you like the flavour of garlic, spear the meaty parts of the lamb with 4–5 slivers of garlic before browning it in oil.

In a large deep casserole heat the oil and brown the lamb on all sides. Remove it, add the onion and carrot, lower the heat, and cook gently for 8–10 minutes until the vegetables are lightly browned. Put back the lamb, add the bouquet garni, rosemary, garlic, salt and pepper, and pour over the wine and stock. Cover, bring to the boil and braise in a moderately low oven (170°C, Mark 3, 325°F) for 2¼–2½ hours or until the lamb is very tender. *You can prepare 48 hours ahead up to this point.*

To reheat the lamb: Discard any solidified fat from the surface of the liquid and cook in a moderately low oven (170°C, Mark 3, 325°F) for about 1 hour or until very hot. Arrange the lamb on a dish and keep warm. Strain the cooking liquid, bring it to the boil, taste for seasoning and serve as a separate gravy.
Garnish dish with watercress just before serving.

Green Peppercorn Sauce

4 egg yolks
salt
225 g/½ lb/1 cup butter
2–3 tbs tarragon vinegar
3–4 tbs water
2 tbs green peppercorns, drained

Green peppercorns are available in tins at specialty food stores. Once opened, they can be kept in an airtight jar in the refrigerator for 1–2 months; drain them before using. The recipe can be doubled easily; if quantities are halved, the hot butter must be added very slowly to the egg yolks.

Put the egg yolks with a little salt in a blender and work at medium speed for 20 seconds. Melt the butter and heat until very hot and bubbling, but do not let it brown. Set the blender at medium speed and add the hot butter very slowly until the mixture starts to thicken, then continue adding it in a steady stream. Add 2 tablespoons vinegar with enough water to make a sauce that pours easily (it tends to stiffen on standing). Add the peppercorns and blend for 10 seconds until they are broken up but not puréed. Taste the sauce, adding more vinegar, peppercorns, or salt if needed, and keep warm or reheat it in a bain-marie.

This sauce should be served warm, not hot. If it gets too hot, it will curdle.

Buttered Green Beans

1 kg/2 lb green beans
salt and pepper
3 tbs butter

Trim the green beans and cut them in half
if large. Cook them in a large kettle of boiling salted water, uncovered, for 15–20
minutes or until tender but still firm. Drain
them and run under cold water to set the
colour. Just before serving, melt the butter
in a pan and toss the beans over high heat
until very hot; add salt and pepper to taste.

Lima Bean Purée

450 g/1 lb/$2\frac{1}{2}$ cups dried lima beans, soaked
    overnight and drained
50 g/2 oz/$\frac{1}{4}$ cup butter
1 onion, finely chopped
juice $\frac{1}{2}$ lemon
$\frac{1}{2}$ tsp ground cumin
$\frac{1}{2}$ tsp ground coriander
salt and freshly ground black pepper

This recipe can easily be halved or doubled.

Cover the beans with water, bring to the
boil and simmer, covered, for 45 minutes or
until very tender; drain them, reserving the
liquid.
    In a pan, heat the butter and fry the
onion until soft but not browned. Add to
the beans and work the mixture through a
sieve or food mill, or purée it in a blender
with a little of the cooking liquid. Return
the purée to the pan and add the lemon
juice, cumin, coriander, and salt and pepper
to taste. Reheat, adding enough of the
reserved cooking liquid to make a mixture
that falls fairly easily from the spoon. Pile in
a serving dish.

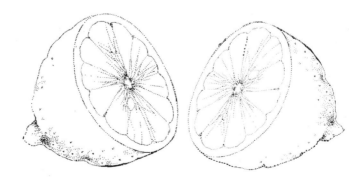

Coffee Charlotte

2½ packages (about 28) sponge fingers
4 tbs rum
250 g/½ lb/1 cup unsalted butter
250 g/½ lb/1 cup sugar
2 tbs dry instant coffee dissolved in 1½ tsp
   water
3.75 dl/¾ pt/1½ cups double cream, whipped
   until it holds a soft peak
1.25 dl/¼ pt/½ cup double cream, stiffly
   whipped (for decoration)
chocolate sauce (for serving)

*charlotte mould or soufflé dish (1½ l/1½-quart
capacity); icing bag and medium star nozzle*

You can halve this recipe easily, but if you
double it, make the charlotte in 2 moulds
rather than 1 large one.

Line the base of the mould or soufflé dish
with a circle of greaseproof paper. Line the
sides with sponge fingers, trimming them so
they fit tightly. Sprinkle remaining sponge
fingers, with 2 tablespoons of the rum.
   In a bowl, cream the butter, gradually
beat in the sugar, and continue beating
until the mixture is light and soft. Beat in
the instant coffee, stir in the remaining 2
tablespoons rum, and then very gently stir
in the lightly whipped cream. *Do not beat in
the cream or it will curdle.* Spoon half the
mixture into the prepared mould, add a
layer of sponge fingers, then add the
remaining mixture. Cover and chill at least
2 hours or until firmly set.
   To serve: Unmould the charlotte onto a
dish. Put the stiffly whipped cream into an
icing bag fitted with the star nozzle and
decorate the top and base of the charlotte
with rosettes of whipped cream. Serve with
cold chocolate sauce.

Cold Chocolate Sauce

225 g/½ lb unsweetened chocolate
1.8 dl/6 fl. oz/¾ cup water
100 g/¼ lb/½ cup sugar
pinch of salt
1 tsp sugar (for sprinkling)
2 tbs rum or brandy

This recipe can be halved or made in up to
four times this amount.

Melt the chocolate in water over low heat,
stirring occasionally. Add the sugar and salt
and stir until melted, then boil steadily for 3
minutes or until the sauce is slightly thickened. Sprinkle the top with the teaspoon of
sugar to prevent a skin from forming and
let cool. Stir in the rum or brandy, cover
tightly and chill.

A Light Summer Buffet

Chicken Elizabeth
Chicken Phillipe
Rice Salad
Green Salad
Fresh Peach Flan

This is an ideal summer buffet for eight, sixteen, or almost any number of people. In fact, the principal recipes were specially designed for large numbers. Chicken Phillipe and chicken Elizabeth were created by the Cordon Bleu Cookery School in London for the banquet served to Queen Elizabeth at her coronation in 1953. Chicken Elizabeth is coated with an unusual mild curry mayonnaise and chicken Phillipe has a garlic-flavoured vinaigrette dressing and a garnish of mushrooms, pink from cooking in port.

The accompaniments are simple but colourful. Rice salad is a refreshing alternative to plain old potato salad and can be served with all kinds of cold meat, fish, and poultry dishes. It is made of boiled rice and diced vegetables, tossed with vinaigrette dressing. Green salad, a favourite at any buffet, is on page 52.

Fresh peach flan makes good use of walnuts, which are ground to give added flavour to a splendidly rich French pastry. The baked pastry shell is filled with fresh peach halves, and the riper the peaches, the better the pie. At other times of year, you can substitute strawberries, stoned cherries, seedless green grapes, or sliced pears for the peaches; red fruits should be glazed with melted redcurrants jelly and white or green fruits with apricot jam glaze.

This buffet menu has another great advantage besides its versatility – almost all preparation can be done ahead. As you can see from the countdown, you need only about an hour to assemble the salads and put the finishing touches to the flan before serving.

And if you decide to multiply this menu to serve large numbers, you can increase the quantities with little extra effort and with few of the usual complications of large-scale cooking – too small pans or ovens and lack of space.

COUNTDOWN

Day Before
Cook chickens and cool. Cut them up
   and keep tightly covered.
Make curry mayonnaise and keep in airtight container.
Cook mushrooms for chicken Phillipe.
Make 5 dl/1 pt/2 cups vinaigrette dressing for chicken Elizabeth garnish,
   chicken Phillipe, rice salad, and green
   salad.
Cook rice for salad, let dry and keep
   covered; prepare vegetables and keep
   in plastic bags.
Wash salad greens and keep in plastic
   bag.
Make and bake walnut pastry pie shells,
   store in airtight container; make
   apricot jam glaze.

In the Morning
Peel tomatoes for chicken Elizabeth and
   cover.
Prepare shallots, garlic, and parsley for
   chicken Phillipe.

2–3 Hours Before Serving
Peel peaches and complete pie; keep at
   room temperature.

¾–1 Hour Before Serving
Mix rice, vegetables, and dressing and
   pile in bowl.
Arrange chickens on platters.
Coat chicken Elizabeth with curry dressing and sprinkle with paprika; add
   tomatoes.
Coat chicken Phillipe with mushroom
   and vinaigrette dressing; add watercress.

Just Before Serving
Toss green salad with dressing.

A Light Summer Buffet

Chicken Elizabeth

1½–2 kg/4–4½ lb roasting chicken
1 large onion, quartered
1 large carrot, quartered
2 stalks celery
bouquet garni
6 peppercorns
½ tsp salt

For the curry mayonnaise
1 tbs oil
1 small onion, finely chopped
2 tsp curry powder
4 tbs tomato juice
4 tbs red wine
2 tbs apricot jam
3.75 dl/¾ pt/1½ cups mayonnaise (page 45)
salt and pepper (optional)

For garnish
½ kg/1 lb small tomatoes, peeled (page 207)
4 tbs vinaigrette dressing (page 41)
little paprika (for sprinkling)

trussing needle and string

On its own, this recipe serves four people,
and it can easily be doubled or tripled to
serve eight or twelve. Together, the recipe
for chicken Elizabeth and chicken Phillipe
yield eight servings.

Truss the chicken (page 208) and set it on
its back in a large saucepan. Surround it
with the onion, carrot, celery, bouquet
garni, peppercorns, and salt, add enough
water to barely cover the thighs, put on the
lid and bring to the boil very slowly.
Simmer 1¼ hours or until no pink juice runs
out when thigh is pierced with a skewer.
Leave to cool slightly in the pan, transfer to
a plate to cool completely, then cover and
chill.

Chicken Phillipe

For the curry mayonnaise: In a saucepan
heat the oil and sauté the onion until soft
but not brown. Add the curry powder and
cook gently 2 minutes. Add the tomato
juice and red wine and simmer until reduced by half. Stir in the apricot jam, let
cool and strain, pressing well to extract the
liquid. Stir this mixture into the mayonnaise
to make a sauce that coats the back of a
spoon. If necessary, add 1 tablespoon warm
water to the mayonnaise to thin it slightly;
taste for seasoning.

Remove trussing strings and cut the
chicken into 8 pieces (page 209). Remove
the skin from the chicken. *You can prepare
24 hours ahead up to this point.*

Not more than an hour before serving
arrange the pieces of chicken along one side
of a platter and coat them with some of the
curry mayonnaise; serve the remaining
mayonnaise separately. Mix the tomatoes
with vinaigrette dressing, and arrange them
on the other side of the platter. Sprinkle a
little paprika on the chicken to add colour.

$1\frac{1}{2}$–2 kg/4–$4\frac{1}{2}$ lb roasting chicken
salt and pepper
2 tsp thyme, tarragon, or rosemary
50 g/2 oz/$\frac{1}{4}$ cup butter, softened
1.25–1.80 dl/4–6 fl. oz/$\frac{1}{2}$–$\frac{3}{4}$ cup stock

For garnish
450 g/1 lb small mushrooms
2 tbs oil
2.5 dl/$\frac{1}{2}$ pt/1 cup port or red wine
2 shallots, finely chopped
2 cloves garlic, crushed
2 tbs chopped parsley
1.25 dl/$\frac{1}{4}$ pt/$\frac{1}{2}$ cup vinaigrette dressing
  (page 41)
bunch of watercress

trussing needle and string

Like chicken Elizabeth, this recipe serves
four people, and it is easy to double, triple,
or make as many times as your oven will
hold chickens.

Set the oven at moderately hot (190°C,
Mark 5, 375°F).

Sprinkle the inside of the chicken with
the salt and pepper, thyme, tarragon, or
rosemary, and truss it (page 208). Spread it
with butter, set on its side in a roasting
pan, and pour around half the stock. Cover
loosely with foil and roast in the heated
oven, turning the chicken onto the other
leg and then onto its back during cooking.
Baste the chicken from time to time during
cooking, adding more stock if the pan is
dry. Remove the foil for the last 15 minutes
of cooking if the chicken is not brown. Cook
for $1\frac{1}{4}$–$1\frac{1}{2}$ hours or until no pink juice runs
from the inside of the bird when it is lifted.

Let it cool in the cooking liquid, then drain and chill until cold.

For garnish: Trim stems of mushrooms and sauté 1–2 minutes in the oil until oil is absorbed. Add port or red wine and boil until the wine is reduced to 2 tablespoons; let cool. *You can prepare 24 hours ahead up to this point.*

A short time before serving, remove the trussing strings from the chicken and carve it into 8 pieces (page 209). Stir shallots, garlic, parsley, and vinaigrette dressing into the mushroom garnish. Arrange the pieces of chicken down one side of a platter and spoon some dressing over them. Arrange the mushrooms and dressing on the other side of the platter and garnish with watercress.

Rice Salad

500 g/1 lb/2 cups rice
salt
2 carrots, diced
1 green sweet pepper, cored, seeded, and diced
1 red sweet pepper, cored, seeded, and diced
225 g/$\frac{1}{2}$ lb/1 cup cooked green peas
2 medium tomatoes, peeled, seeded, and cut into strips (page 207)
3 stalks celery, thinly sliced
1.8 dl/6 fl. oz/$\frac{3}{4}$ cup vinaigrette dressing (page 41)
freshly ground black pepper (optional)

This recipe is easy to halve or multiply, but do not cook more than 1$\frac{1}{2}$ kg/3 lb of rice (to serve 24) at one time. If some vegetables are not available, you can omit them, but try always to include a variety since contrasting colours are part of the attraction of the salad.

Cook the rice in plenty of boiling salted water for 10–12 minutes or until just tender. Drain it in a colander, rinse with hot water to wash away the starch, poke a few drainage holes with the handle of a spoon, and leave in the colander for 10–15 minutes to dry.

Cook the carrots in boiling salted water for 8–10 minutes or until tender and drain. Blanch the green and red peppers in boiling salted water for 1 minute, drain, refresh with cold water, and drain thoroughly. *You can prepare 24 hours ahead up to this point.*

Not more than an hour before serving, mix the carrots, peppers, peas, tomatoes, and celery carefully with the rice, add the dressing and mix well; taste for seasoning and pile in a bowl.

Fresh Peach Flan

2.5/½ pt/1 cup apricot jam glaze (see
   next recipe)
7–8 ripe peaches, peeled, halved, and stoned
   (page 208)

For walnut pastry
75 g/3 oz/¾ cup walnut pieces
350 g/¾ lb/3 cups flour
pinch of salt
1 tsp ground cinnamon
175 g/6 oz/¾ cup butter, softened
175 g/6 oz/¾ cup sugar
2 eggs
½ tsp vanilla extract

two 25 cm/9-inch flan rings or deep pie pans

This recipe makes two pies. The pastry pro-
portions are difficult to halve, but dough left
over if you make only one pie is delicious
for biscuits. To double the quantities, make
2 batches of pastry. Be sure to use freestone
peaches as clingstone fruits are hard to
stone.

Grind the walnuts a few at a time in a
blender or work them through a rotary
cheese grater. Sift the flour, salt, and cinnamon onto a board or marble slab, add the
walnuts, and make a large well in the
centre. Put the butter, sugar, eggs, and
vanilla into the well, and work with the
fingertips until well mixed. Gradually draw
in the flour, using the whole hand, and
knead the dough with the heel of the hand
until smooth and it peels easily from the
board in one piece. Wrap and chill at least
30 minutes.

Set the oven at moderately hot (190°C,
Mark 5, 375°F). Divide the dough in half,
roll it out, and line both flan rings or pie
pans. Line shells with greaseproof paper and
beans and bake empty as for a regular pie
pastry shell (page 51). Shells may be baked
up to 24 hours ahead and kept in airtight
containers.

Melt the apricot jam glaze and brush the
inside of the pie shells, *This helps prevent the
pastry from becoming soggy*. Arrange the
peach halves as close together as possible in
the shells, cut sides down, and brush generously with glaze, filling it into all corners.
Serve within 3–4 hours.

Apricot Jam Glaze

In a pan melt 1 jar (350 g/¾ lb) apricot jam
with the juice of ½ lemon and 2 tablespoons
water. Work through a strainer and store in
an airtight jar. Reheat before using; makes
about 3.25 dl/¾ pt/1½ cups.

A Sophisticated Supper

Cheese Soufflé
Stuffed Beef Chasseur
Touraine Potatoes
Green Salad
Meringue Petits Fours and Coffee

Hearty stuffed beef chasseur is the centre-piece for this French-inspired menu which begins with one of the glories of Gallic cooking – a cheese soufflé – and ends with one of the easiest-to-make desserts – a confection of little meringues.

This cheese soufflé is superbly light and delicate. Unlike some soufflés that take almost an hour to bake, it is cooked – in true French tradition – for only 10–12

minutes in a hot oven. The finished soufflé is crisp and brown on the outside with a soft, creamy centre, that forms a sauce over the rest. Such a dish is heaven-sent if there are tardy guests, because it can go into the oven after they arrive. As with most soufflés, care must be taken in the making, but all danger points are marked in the instructions. For best results, use a copper bowl and a balloon whisk to beat the egg whites; instructions are on page 208.

Another French classic is the stuffed beef chasseur. *Chasseur* means hunter, and the name alludes to ingredients such as mushrooms which hunters found in the woods and fields. A white wine and tomato-flavoured sauce finishes this dish. Serve it with Touraine potatoes, whose simple seasonings of salt, pepper, and parsley, provide a pleasant contrast to the vigour of the main dish. Green salad (page 52) is also an excellent accompaniment.

The meringues for the petits fours can be baked several days ahead and stored in an airtight container before decorating and serving with coffee. Half are topped with strawberries and the rest are sandwiched with uncooked meringue mixture – a trick familiar to professional chefs. The meringue is made by thoroughly beating icing sugar with egg whites so it is stiff enough to be kept in the refrigerator for up to a week without separating. It can be baked, like regular meringue, or used uncooked in fillings and to sweeten whipped cream.

COUNTDOWN

1–2 Days Before

Stuff and cook beef; leave ready for reheating in casserole.

Make meringues, but do not sandwich
nut meringues, and arrange on a dish
strawberries; store in an airtight container.

Store meringue filling in a jar in refrigerator.

Day Before

Wash lettuce for salad and keep in plastic bag; make dressing.

1–2 Hours Before Supper

Finish strawberry meringues, sandwich
nut meringues, and arrange on a dish.

Make cheese mixture for soufflé and prepare soufflé dish; leave the unbeaten
egg whites at room temperature.

Parboil potatoes.

30 Minutes Before Supper

Set oven at hot (220°C, Mark 7, 425°F)
for soufflé.

20 Minutes Before Supper

Set beef on low heat to reheat.

15 Minutes Before Supper

Beat egg whites, complete soufflé, and
bake.

Fry potatoes.

When soufflé is cooked, turn oven to low
(130°C, Mark $\frac{1}{2}$, 250°F) and keep beef
and potatoes hot.

After Serving Soufflé

Transfer beef to a dish, remove strings,
and spoon over garnish; serve sauce
separately.

Sprinkle potatoes with parsley and
seasoning.

Toss salad.

Cheese Soufflé

3.25 dl/$\frac{3}{4}$ pt/1$\frac{1}{2}$ cups double cream
1$\frac{1}{2}$ tbs potato starch
1$\frac{1}{2}$ tbs butter
8 eggs, separated
50 g/2 oz/$\frac{3}{4}$ cup grated Parmesan cheese
75 g/3 oz/$\frac{3}{4}$ cup grated Gruyère cheese
salt and pepper
pinch dry mustard
5 egg whites

*2 soufflé dishes (1$\frac{1}{2}$ l/3 pt/1$\frac{1}{2}$-quart capacity
each)*

This recipe can be halved to serve three to
four people; do not try to double it because
the egg whites are too difficult to beat.

Set the oven at hot (220°C, Mark 7, 425°F).
Thickly butter the soufflé dishes. Tie a foil
or greaseproof paper collar around them to
extend 6–8 cm/2–3 inches above the rim;
butter the collars.

In a heavy saucepan, put the cream,
potato starch, and butter, and heat gently,
stirring, until the sauce thickens. *Take at
once from the heat or the sauce will separate.*
Stir in the 8 egg yolks and cheese, reserving
2 tablespoons Gruyère cheese to sprinkle on
top of the soufflé. Heat gently, stirring until
the mixture thickens slightly again. *Do not
overcook it or the cheese will form strings.*
Take from the heat and add salt and pepper
and mustard. The mixture should be highly
seasoned to compensate for the bland egg
whites. *You can prepare 2 hours ahead up to
this point.* Let the egg whites come to room
temperature. If preparing in advance, cover
the surface of the sauce with wet greaseproof paper to prevent a skin from forming.

To finish the soufflés: Stiffly whip the 13

egg whites, if possible using a copper bowl (page 208). *Be sure the egg whites, bowl, and beater are free from moisture and egg yolks or the whites will not whip properly.* Heat the cheese mixture until it is hot to the touch. Add about a quarter of the egg whites and stir until well mixed – this cooks the egg whites slightly and lightens the mixture. Add this mixture to the remaining egg whites and fold together as carefully as possible. Pour the mixture into the prepared soufflé dishes – it should fill them almost to the brim – sprinkle with the reserved cheese and bake in the heated oven for 10–12 minutes or until the soufflés are puffed and brown. Remove the foil or paper collar and serve at once.

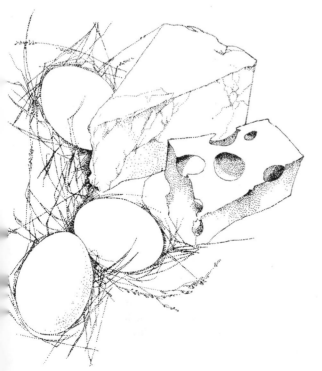

Stuffed Beef Chasseur

2 rump steaks (about 700 g/1½ lb each)
2 tbs oil
1 onion, chopped
1 tbs flour
5 dl/1 pt/2 cups white wine
2.5 dl/½ pt/1 cup stock
1 tbs tomato paste
bouquet garni
salt and pepper
350 g/¾ lb mushrooms
3 tomatoes, peeled, seeded, and cut in strips (page 207)

For the stuffing
450 g/1 lb sausage meat
1 onion, finely chopped
2 shallots or spring onions, finely chopped
1 tbs chopped parsley
1 egg, beaten to mix
salt and pepper
6 slices bacon

You can happily double this recipe.

Cut the steaks in half lengthwise with the knife parallel to the board.

To make the stuffing: Mix the sausage meat with the onion, shallots or spring onions, parsley, egg, and plenty of salt and pepper. Spread all but one slice of steak with stuffing and lay 2 slices of bacon on top of each slice. Stack the layers like a sandwich, reversing some slices so the pile is even in height. Top with the plain slice and tie the meat with string at 5 cm/2-inch intervals to form a roll.

In a casserole, heat the oil and brown the meat on all sides. Take out, add the onion and cook gently until soft. Stir in the flour and cook, stirring, until well browned. Pour in the wine, stock, tomato paste, bouquet garni, salt and pepper, and bring to the boil. Replace the meat, cover and cook in a moderately low oven (170°C, Mark 3, 325°F) for $1\frac{1}{2}$-2 hours or until a skewer inserted into the meat for 1 minute is hot to the touch when withdrawn.

Trim the mushroom stems level with the caps and quarter them, if large. Add the mushrooms to the casserole. *You can prepare 2 days ahead up to this point.* Keep meat and sauce in the refrigerator.

If serving at once, continue cooking 10 minutes; add tomatoes and cook 5 minutes more. If beef was prepared ahead, reheat it over low heat on top of stove or heat in a moderate oven (180°C, Mark 4, 350°F) for 25–35 minutes or until very hot; add tomatoes and continue cooking 5 minutes more.

Lift out the meat, remove the strings, and set the meat on a serving dish. Discard the bouquet garni and skim the sauce, if necessary. Spoon over the mushroom and tomato garnish with a little sauce and serve the remaining sauce separately. For serving, carve the meat in vertical slices $1\,cm/\frac{1}{2}$ inch thick.

Touraine Potatoes

6–8 large potatoes
$100\,g/\frac{1}{4}\,lb/\frac{1}{2}$ cup butter
1 tbs chopped parsley
salt and pepper

This recipe can easily be halved, but double quantity is difficult to deal with.

Cut the potatoes in $2-2\frac{1}{2}\,cm/\frac{3}{4}$-1-inch cubes. Parboil them in boiling salted water for 3 minutes and drain.

A short time before serving, heat the butter in a pan and fry the potatoes 5–7 minutes over medium heat, turning them occasionally so they brown on several sides. Transfer to a serving dish and sprinkle with parsley, salt and pepper.

Six O'Clock Supper. A simple meal for two opens with melon and grape salad, followed by baked aubergine and pork chops with a cheese topping

Meringue Petits Fours

For the meringue
450 g/1 lb/3 cups icing sugar
6 egg whites

To finish
60 walnut or pecan halves
2 tsp dry instant coffee dissolved in $\frac{1}{2}$ tsp
　water
100 g/$\frac{1}{4}$ lb/$\frac{1}{2}$ cup redcurrant jelly
15 small strawberries, halved through the
　stem

icing bag and medium star nozzle

This recipe makes about 30 nut meringues
and 30 strawberry meringues. You can
halve it easily, but to double, make 2
batches of meringue.

Set the oven at low (150°C, Mark 2, 300°F);
grease a baking sheet and sprinkle it with
icing sugar, discarding the excess.

To make the meringue: Sift the measured
icing sugar. Beat the egg whites until frothy
and beat in the sugar a tablespoon at a
time. If beating by hand, set the bowl over
a pan of simmering water and continue
beating until the mixture holds a stiff peak
when the beater is lifted; take from the heat
and continue beating until cool. If you are
using an electric beater, no heat is necessary.

Put the meringue in an icing bag fitted
with a medium star nozzle and pipe about
half the mixture into rosettes, leaving a
hollow in the centre. Pipe $\frac{1}{4}$ of the remaining mixture into small mounds, and top
each one with a walnut or pecan half. Bake
the petits fours in the heated oven for 30
minutes or until crisp and lightly browned.
Transfer them to a rack to cool.

Flavour the remaining meringue with
coffee to taste. *You can prepare 1–2 days
ahead up to this point.* Store petits fours in an
airtight container and coffee-flavoured
meringue in a jar in the refrigerator.

A few hours before serving: Melt the redcurrant jelly and stir until smooth. Dip each
strawberry half in jelly to coat it and set it,
rounded side up, in the middle of a
meringue rosette. Sandwich the nut
meringues with a little of the coffee
meringue mixture.

Dinner for All Seasons. French inspiration shows
in this menu of spicy mushrooms and onions à
la Grecque, braised leg of lamb served with a
green peppercorn sauce, and the dessert of coffee
charlotte

A Hearty Breakfast

Fresh Melon or Grapefruit
Baked Eggs Basquaise
Devilled Kidneys in Bacon
American Fruit Muffins
Coffee or Tea

The sharp refreshing flavours of fresh fruits are as bracing in the morning as a well-brewed cup of coffee. Grapefruit and melon are old favourites, or you might like to turn for a change to such exotic fruits as papaya (at its best with a squeeze of lime juice) or a slice of fresh pineapple topped with strawberries. Fresh fruits like strawberries, bananas, and blackberries, blackcurrants or raspberries will also liven up muffins. When blackberries, or blackcurrants are out of season, you can substitute frozen ones, taken straight from the package without defrosting.

If you have not tried them before, American muffins are quick but quirky to make. The batter should be stirred until it is only just mixed and still looks rough, then baked and served at once. Otherwise your muffins will have a solid texture and a depressed look that is hardly encouraging at the start of the day. Be sure to serve them while still warm.

Eggs Basquaise are an ocean away from American muffins, but they come together remarkably well. The Basque people live in the valleys of the northern Pyrenees, and their cooking is a blend of French and Spanish. They are famous for omelettes and these baked eggs Basquaise flavoured with ham and green pepper. The ham should be a lightly smoked country type, like that from the Basque city of Bayonne.

Devilled kidneys used to be a breakfast favourite. Marinated in spices, they are rolled in bacon and then grilled until the bacon is crisp but the kidneys are still rare in the centre. Kidneys cooked in this way are also an excellent supper dish served on toast or with rice pilaf.

Breakfast would not be breakfast without coffee, and with the inexpensive electric coffee grinders now available, you can experiment with blending different kinds of beans to get the brew you want. Also try blending your own mixture of Indian and China tea and remember the best is made by pouring boiling water over the tea in an already warmed pot. This breakfast calls for one extra touch – unsalted butter curls for the muffins. Simply draw a serrated knife gently lengthwise down a stick of butter and pile the curls into a small dish.

COUNTDOWN

Evening Before
Prepare grapefruit and keep tightly
    covered; chill melon.
Cook ham and pepper mixture for eggs
    Basquaise and cover.
Prepare kidneys and leave to marinate in
    devil mixture.
Prepare fruit for muffins.

45 Minutes Before Breakfast
Set oven at hot (220°C, Mark 7, 425°F).
Make muffins and bake.
Prepare melon.

25 Minutes Before Breakfast
Prepare kidney rolls.
Assemble eggs Basquaise.

10–15 Minutes Before Breakfast
Make coffee.
Take out muffins and keep warm; turn
    oven to moderate (180°C, Mark 4,
    350°F).
Bake eggs.
Grill or fry kidney rolls.
Make tea.

Baked Eggs Basquaise

50 g/2 oz/$\frac{1}{4}$ cup butter
2 large onions, sliced
2 thick slices (about 700 g/1$\frac{1}{2}$ lb) cooked
    ham, diced
2 green peppers, cored, seeded, and cut in
    strips
salt and freshly ground black pepper
2 tbs chopped parsley
16 eggs

*eight 10–15 cm/4–5-inch diameter gratin or
    individual baking dishes*

This recipe can easily be halved, quartered,
or doubled. If you don't have individual
baking dishes, use one large shallow dish.

Set the oven at moderate (180°C, Mark 4,
350°F). In a frying pan, heat the butter and
sauté the onions until soft but not browned.
Add the ham and continue cooking until
onion and ham are lightly browned. Add
the green peppers with salt and pepper and
cook until soft. Stir in the parsley and taste
for seasoning. *The mixture should be well
seasoned to balance the unseasoned eggs, but
beware of adding too much salt with the ham.
You can prepare 12 hours ahead up to this
point.*
    Just before baking, butter the gratin
dishes and spread the mixture in them,
making one hollow for each egg. Break the
eggs into the baking dishes and bake in the
heated oven for 8–18 minutes or until the
egg whites are set but the yolks are still
soft. *The flatter the dish, the shorter the baking
time.* Serve at once with the kidneys in
bacon on the same dish.

Devilled Kidneys in Bacon

8 lamb kidneys
16 slices (about 450 g / 1 lb bacon, cut in
  half)

For devil mixture
1 tbs ketchup
2 tsp Worcestershire sauce
2 tsp soy sauce
1 tsp sugar
½ tsp cayenne
½ tsp pepper
½ tsp ground ginger
½ tsp dry mustard

8 kebab skewers (optional)

This recipe can be doubled or halved; if you
serve it as a lunch or supper dish, allow
1½–2 kidneys per person.

Cut the core from the kidneys with scissors
or a sharp knife and cut each one in equal
quarters. In a bowl mix the ketchup,
Worcestershire, and soy sauces, sugar,
cayenne, pepper, ginger and mustard; add
the kidneys and toss until well coated.
Cover and let stand in the refrigerator for at
least 3 and up to 12 hours.

  A short time before serving, heat the grill,
if used. Roll each piece of kidney in half a
strip of bacon, and if you wish thread four
rolls on each kebab skewer. Grill 5 minutes
each side or fry over fairly high heat until
the bacon is browned. If using skewers, set
one over each dish of eggs Basquaise, pull
the kidney rolls off the skewers with a fork
and serve; otherwise remove the kidney
rolls from the grill pan or frying pan with a
slotted spoon and place four rolls on each
dish of eggs.

American Fruit Muffins

100 g / ¼ lb / 2 cups prepared blackcurrants,
  raspberries, blackberries, strawberries, or
  bananas (see below)
500 g / 18 oz / 4 cups flour
100 g / ¼ lb / ⅓ cup sugar
1 level tbs baking powder
1 tsp salt
2 eggs, beaten to mix
100 g / ¼ lb / ½ cup melted butter
2.5 dl / ½ pt / 2 cups milk

bun tins for 24 muffins

This recipe makes 24 muffins; it can be
halved, but don't try to double it.

Prepare the fruit: Pick over and wash blackcurrants, blackberries or raspberries; hull
and cut strawberries in chunks; mash
bananas to a smooth pulp. Grease muffin
tins and set oven at hot (220°C, Mark 7,
425°F).

  Sift flour with sugar, baking powder, and
salt into a bowl. Make a well in the centre
and add the eggs, butter, and milk. Stir
with a wooden spoon quickly and lightly
until flour is just moistened. Add fruit and
stir until just mixed – *the batter should still
be slightly rough.* Spoon it into the prepared
tins and bake in the heated oven for 25–30
minutes or until browned. Serve while still
warm.

MENUS
FOR TEN

A Gourmet Picnic

A Winter Buffet

An Elegant Lunch

Dinner in a Hurry

MENUS FOR TEN

Some cooks become nervous at the idea of cooking for as many as ten people. But with forethought and one or two helpful friends, you can easily prepare and serve an informal meal by yourself and still play the part of the perfect host. For a simple dinner, you may like to compromise by leaving guests to serve themselves buffet-style, while assigning them places at the table. However, for a formal dinner with several changes of plates and more than one wine, you will need someone to serve or you will be rushed off your feet.

A picnic will pose no such problem. In keeping with the outdoors, this Gourmet Picnic has the sun-soaked appeal of southern France. Two dishes on the menu – salade Niçoise and ratatouille – are Provençal specialities, and they are preceded by a country terrine flavoured with ham and pistachios and served with a simple whole wheat bread. All these dishes go well with a light red wine like a Beaujolais, or a rosé from Provence.

Turning from sun to snow, add warmth to the season with a Winter Buffet, centred on cassoulet – a sumptuous stew of baked beans with bacon, pork, lamb, duck, tomatoes, and onions that is a speciality of south western France. With it comes tarte Tatin, a delectable upside-down apple pie – the pride of Maxim's restaurant in Paris, Such dishes demand a hearty red wine – for preference a Burgundy or something from the Côtes du Rhône.

An Elegant Lunch that can be prepared ahead appeals at any season. Individual mushroom tartlets, puffed up like soufflés, are followed by chicken that is baked with Parma ham to give it a distinctive smoky tang. The melting richness of petits pots de crème – baked custards in a variety of flavours – makes an excellent ending.

To produce a Dinner in a Hurry for ten is quite a feat if you have only a few hours' warning, but it can be done with the dishes in this menu. Oyster soup, pork tenderloin with a mushroom, walnut, and celery garnish, followed by hot raspberry soufflé, demand only an hour or so of your time in the morning or the day before, plus a half hour before the party.

For more formal ideas, turn to the Summer and Winter Dinners in Menus for Twelve. The summer menu, of pigeon in wine sauce with grapes, includes iced cucumber soup and peaches cardinal with a raspberry sauce. For winter, chestnut soup is followed by roast veal Orloff, layered with mushroom purée and ham and coated with cream sauce – a classic French dish that can be made ahead and reheated. You can keep the same quantities for all these recipes (with the exception of the pigeon) since the difference between serving ten and twelve people is so small.

A Gourmet Picnic

Country Terrine
Salade Niçoise
Ratatouille
Whole Wheat Bread
Fresh Peaches or Pears
Port Salut or Gruyère
Cheese

There is something irresistible about picnicking. Food tastes better and drinks are more refreshing outdoors despite such drawbacks as sunburn, insects, and lack of running water. This gourmet picnic is portable as well as palatable, and all the dishes will survive without refrigeration for several hours.

Country terrine is a hearty, well-spiced mixture of pork, veal, and chicken liver, layered with ham and studded with pistachios. It is baked, in classic fashion, in a special mould also called a terrine that has a close-fitting lid. The mould is filled to the brim with the mixture, and the lid is sealed on with a flour and water paste, called luting paste, so no flavour is lost by evaporation.

Terrines come in all shapes, sizes, and materials, from decorated heat-proof porcelain or simple earthenware to enamelled cast iron. All are equally good, provided they are thick and conduct the heat evenly. Mixtures cooked in a long, narrow terrine, shaped like an extended loaf of bread, are easy to cut in slices for serving, but remember that they will cook more quickly than in a rectangular or oval mould.

The two salads served with the terrine are based on vegetables like tomatoes, aubergine, green beans, courgettes and peppers that won't wilt in the heat. For a picnic, both the salads and the terrine look their best in plain earthenware pottery containers.

Any ripe fresh fruit will go well with this menu. Peaches, pears, plums, or strawberries are obvious choices, but figs or pomegranates would add an exotic touch. The cheese should be hard, or only semisoft, both to stand up to the heat and to hold its own with the other strong flavours on the menu. For example, Port Salut, cherry or walnut-flavoured gourmandise, or a well-aged Gruyère would all be excellent.

The bread to go with the terrine, and afterward with the cheese, is unusual in that it is mixed only very lightly, instead of being kneaded for several minutes like most yeast breads. It has a light, slightly crumbly texture and is made with stone-ground flour, which gives it a nutty flavour that is the perfect foil to the other hearty dishes in this menu.

COUNTDOWN

Several Days Before
Make terrine.
Make bread and freeze.

Day Before
Make ratatouille.
Cook green beans for salade Niçoise; slice
    cucumbers, peel tomatoes, and keep
    covered. Prepare anchovies and olives;
    make dressing.
Take bread from freezer and let thaw.

In the Morning
Complete salad Niçoise.
Pack cheese, fruit, and drinks to carry.

Country Terrine

450 g/1 lb sliced bacon
2 tbs butter
2 onions, chopped
1 kg/2 lb pork (half fat, half lean), minced
450 g/1 lb veal, minced
450 g/1 lb chicken livers, finely chopped
3 cloves garlic, crushed
$\frac{1}{2}$ tsp ground allspice
$\frac{1}{4}$ tsp ground cloves
$\frac{1}{4}$ tsp ground nutmeg
3 eggs, beaten to mix
2.5 dl/$\frac{1}{2}$ pt/1 cup double cream
4 tbs brandy
salt and freshly ground black pepper
100 g/$\frac{1}{4}$ lb/1 cup shelled pistachios
    (optional)
2 slices cooked ham 3 mm/$\frac{1}{4}$-inch thick
    (about 350 g/$\frac{3}{4}$ lb), cut in strips
2 bay leaves

For luting paste
50 g/2 oz/$\frac{1}{2}$ cup flour
4–5 tbs water

*terrine or casserole with tight-fitting lid
(4 l/8 pt capacity)*

This quantity can be halved or doubled to
bake in 2 terrines. If possible, the terrine
should have an airhole so the mixture can
be tested with a skewer without removing
the lid.

Line the terrine or casserole with bacon,
reserving a few slices for the top.
    Melt the butter in a frying pan and sauté
the onion until soft but not brown. Mix the
onion with the pork, veal, chicken livers,
garlic, allspice, cloves, nutmeg, eggs, cream,
brandy, and plenty of salt and pepper – *the*

mixture should taste very spicy, but do not swallow any because it contains raw pork. Stir in the pistachios, if used. Spread a third of the mixture in the lined terrine, add a layer of half the ham strips, and top with another third of the pork mixture. Add the remaining ham and cover with the last third of the pork. Lay the reserved bacon slices on top, trimming the edges if necessary; set the bay leaves on top of the bacon and add the lid. Set the oven at moderate (180°C, Mark 4, 350°F).

For the luting paste: Mix the flour with the water to a soft paste. *Do not overmix or the paste will become elastic.* Seal the gap around the terrine lid with paste and set the terrine in a roasting pan half filled with hot water (a bain marie). Bring to the boil on top of the stove, then transfer to the oven and cook for $1\frac{3}{4}$–2 hours or until a skewer or wire inserted through the hole in the lid into the centre of the terrine mixture for $\frac{1}{2}$ minute is hot to the touch when withdrawn. If the lid has no hole, lift it to test the terrine. Leave the terrine covered until cool.

Remove the lid, set a plate with a 1-kg/2-lb weight on top and chill for several hours or overnight. Remove the weight and replace the lid. The terrine is best kept for 3–4 days or up to a week so the flavour matures. Carry and serve the terrine in the mould.

Salade Niçoise

1 tin anchovy fillets
3–4 tbs milk
2 tins (200 g/7 oz each) tuna in oil, drained and flaked
700 g/$1\frac{1}{2}$ lb green beans, cooked and drained (page 86)
2 cucumbers, peeled and very thinly sliced
50 g/2 oz/$\frac{1}{2}$ cup black French or Italian-style olives, halved and stoned
450 g/ lb tomatoes, peeled (page 207)

For the dressing
3 tbs lemon juice
1–2 cloves garlic, crushed (depending on individual taste)
salt and freshly ground black pepper
approx. 2.5 dl/$\frac{1}{2}$ pt/$\frac{3}{4}$–1 cup olive oil

This salad is best made several hours in advance so the ingredients have time to marinate in the dressing. Quantities can be halved or doubled.

Halve the anchovies lengthwise and soak in the milk for 10–15 minutes to remove some of the salt; drain.

For the dressing: Whisk the lemon juice and garlic with salt and pepper until the salt dissolves. Whisk in the oil, a little at a time so the dressing emulsifies and thickens slightly. The amount of oil needed depends on the acidity of the lemon juice and the fruitiness of the oil.

Spread the tuna in a large shallow serving dish or salad bowl and cover with the green beans. Moisten with 3–4 table-spoons of the dressing. Cover with the cucumber, overlapping the slices to form a flat layer completely covering the beans. Spoon over 3–4 tablespoons of the remaining dressing and arrange the anchovy fillets in a lattice pattern on top. Put an olive half, rounded side up, in the centre of each lattice. Arrange the tomatoes around the edge of the salad and brush them with the remaining dressing. Cover the salad tightly and leave 3–4 hours or a maximum of 8 hours before serving. Keep it in the refrigerator, but bring to room temperature before serving. Carry and serve in the dish or bowl.

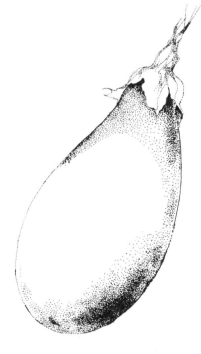

Ratatouille

2 medium aubergines (about 450 g/1 lb), halved and cut in 1-cm/⅔-inch slices
450 g/1 lb small courgettes, cut in 1-cm/½-inch slices
1.25 dl/¼ pt/½ cup olive oil
3 medium onions, thinly sliced
3 red or green peppers, cored, seeded, and sliced
3 cloves garlic, crushed
2 tsp basil
1 tsp thyme
1 tsp ground coriander
¼ tsp aniseed, crushed
salt and freshly ground black pepper
4 large tomatoes, peeled, seeded, and chopped (page 207) or 450 g/1 lb/2 cups tinned tomatoes, drained and chopped
2 tbs chopped parsley (for sprinkling)

This recipe can easily be halved; if you double it, you will get the best results by cooking it in two casseroles or, if you use one large casserole, by cooking it in the oven at a higher heat (200°C, Mark 6, 400°F). The flavour or ratatouille improves if it is made a day or two ahead.

Sprinkle the aubergines and courgettes with salt and let stand 30 minutes. *This draws out the bitter juices.* Drain them, rinse with cold water and drain on paper towels. If using the oven, set it at moderately hot (190°C, Mark 6, 375°F).

In a pan, heat 2 tablespoons oil and fry the onions until soft but not brown. Layer the onions, aubergines, courgettes, and peppers in a casserole (to cook on top of the stove) or in a baking dish (to cook in the oven), sprinkling the garlic, basil, thyme, coriander, aniseed, salt and pepper between the layers. Spoon the remaining oil on top. Cover and simmer on top of the stove, or cook in the heated oven for 20–25 minutes. Add the tomatoes, stir well, and continue cooking 20–25 minutes longer or until the vegetables are tender. *Do not overcook or the vegetables will become soft and unappetizing.* If they produce a great deal of liquid, remove the lid for the last 15 minutes of cooking. Serve hot or cold, sprinkled with parsley. Carry and serve in the baking dish or casserole.

Whole Wheat Bread

1¼ kg/2½ lb/8¾ cups stone-ground whole wheat flour
1 tbs salt
7.5 dl/1¼ pt/3 cups warm water
1½ tbs honey
1½ packages dry or 1½ cakes compressed yeast, 30 g/1 oz fresh yeast or 15 g/½ oz dried yeast

3 medium (22 × 11½ × 6 cm/8½ × 4½ × 2½ inch) loaf tins

You can halve this quantity of bread, but if you double it, you will do best to make 2 batches. Have all the ingredients at room temperature, if possible. The bread keeps fresh for about 12 hours in the refrigerator, or it can be frozen.

Grease the loaf tins. Put the flour in a bowl with the salt and make a well in the centre. Pour in 1.25 dl/¼ pt/½ cup of the warm water and the honey and sprinkle or crumble over the yeast. Let stand in a warm place for 5 minutes or until dissolved. Add nearly all the remaining water and stir gently with the hand until the dough is just mixed. If necessary, add more water – the dough should be so wet that it is slippery. *Unlike most bread doughs, this must be mixed very lightly, not kneaded.* Spoon the dough into the prepared pans, cover with a damp cloth, and let rise in a warm place to the top of the pans (the dough will be almost doubled in bulk). Set the oven at moderately hot (190°C, Mark 5, 375°F).
    Bake the loaves in the heated oven for 50–60 minutes or until they sound hollow when tapped on the bottom. Turn out on a wire rack to cool.

A Winter Buffet

Black and Green Olives
Cassoulet Toulousaine
Tomatoes Provençale
Escarole Salad
Apple Tartes Tatin

Cassoulet is one of the great classics of French cuisine. *Larousse Gastronomique*, the dictionary of French cooking, devotes almost two pages to the dish and describes three versions – from Castelnaudary, Carcassonne, and Toulouse, all towns in the Languedoc region of south western France. For at least a hundred years writers on food have debated the proper constituents of the various versions, and there seems to be general agreement that cassoulet de Castelnaudary is the original, containing dried beans, tomatoes, ham, pork, bacon rind, sausage, and seasonings. To this, Carcassonne adds cubed leg of lamb and, in the hunting season, partridge. The version from Toulouse is the most elaborate and includes shoulder or neck of mutton with the fresh garlic sausages of Toulouse and goose preserved in its fat (*confit d'oie*).

It may be difficult to obtain all the ingredients for an authentic French cassoulet, but a remarkably savoury stew results from following the original recipe with a few substitutions such as fresh duck for preserved goose. Cassoulet is ideal fare for a buffet – easy to reheat, easy to serve, and attractive to look at in its traditional brown earthenware pot. It is complete in itself, but you may like to add tomatoes Provençale, baked with a garlic topping, and a salad of escarole, also known as Batavian endive, with a mustard cream dressing that perfectly complements the slightly peppery bite of this vegetable.

To serve with drinks before the entrée, offer salty Mediterranean French or Italian olives to complete the French country theme.

Dessert is the most aristocratic of apple pies, Tarte des Demoiselles Tatin, It is named after two impoverished gentlewomen from the province of Orléans, who were forced to earn their living by baking their father's favourite apple pie. When turned upside-down for serving, the pie glistens with a layer of caramel absorbed by the apples from the base of the pan in which it is cooked. The apples are sliced and arranged in the pan to interlock like bricks so the pie does not collapse, then covered with a crumbly crust of sweet French pie pastry, that becomes the base of the pie when it is turned out. The caramel topping is the trickiest part – if it is cooked too little, it tastes insipid; if cooked too much it quickly burns.

COUNTDOWN

3 Days Before
Soak beans for cassoulet.

2 Days Before
Make cassoulet and keep covered.

Day Before
Wash escarole and keep in plastic bag;
    make dressing.
Make pastry for tartes Tatin.

In the Morning
Prepare tomatoes but do not bake.
Make and bake tartes Tatin; leave in
    pans for reheating.

2 Hours Before Serving
Set oven at moderately hot (190°C, Mark
    5, 375°F).

1½ Hours Before Serving
Put cassoulet in oven to reheat.
Whip cream for tartes or put sour cream
    in a serving bowl.
Put olives in bowls.

15 Minutes Before Serving
Put tomatoes in oven to bake.
Toss salad.
Take out cassoulet, turn oven to low and
    warm tartes Tatin.

After Serving Cassoulet
Turn out tartes Tatin.

Cassoulet Toulousaine

1 kg/2 lb dried white Great Northern beans
1 carrot, quartered
1 onion, stuck with a clove
2 bouquets garnis
350 g/¾ lb piece salt pork
two 1½–2 kg/3½–4 lb ducks
2 tbs bacon dripping or lard
675 g/1½ lb boned shoulder of lamb, cut into
    2½-cm/1-inch cubes
675 g/1½ lb boneless pork loin cut in 2½-
    cm/1-inch cubes
2 onions chopped
4 cloves garlic, crushed
salt and freshly ground black pepper
450 g/1 lb Toulouse or other fresh garlic
    sausage
4 tomatoes, peeled, seeded, and chopped or
    450 g/1 lb/2 cups tinned tomatoes,
    drained and chopped
50 g/2 oz/½ cup browned breadcrumbs

You can halve this quantity of cassoulet or
double it if you have a large enough casserole. The flavour improves if it is made 2
or 3 days ahead.

Soak the beans overnight in plenty of cold
water and drain them. Put them in a large
pan with the carrot, onion stuck with a
clove, a bouquet garni, salt pork, and water
to cover. Simmer 3 hours or until the beans
burst if you lift out a few in a spoon and
blow on them. Drain them, discarding the
onion, carrot, and bouquet garni; reserve
the salt pork and the cooking liquid.

   Cut each duck in 6 pieces, leaving the
legs in 1 piece (page 209). In a casserole or
pan, heat the bacon dripping or lard, and
brown the duck pieces on all sides, allowing
10–15 minutes so the fat thoroughly dis-

solves. Take out the duck, pour off all but 2 tablespoons of fat, add the lamb and brown also. Take out, add the pork and brown it too. Take out, add the chopped onion and brown it lightly.

In a very large baking dish or casserole, layer the beans with the duck, lamb, pork, onions, garlic, salt and pepper. Add a bouquet garni, set the salt pork on top, moisten with some of the reserved bean liquid, cover and simmer very slowly on top of the stove or bake in a low oven (150°C, Mark 2, 300°F) for 3 hours, adding more liquid during cooking if the mixture becomes dry. Add the garlic sausage and continue cooking 1 hour.

In a pan, crush the tomatoes, adding salt and pepper to fresh ones, and simmer them until pulpy. Take the salt pork and sausage out of the cassoulet, slice them, and replace them. Add the tomato mixture to the casserole, shake to mix, taste for seasoning, and sprinkle the breadcrumbs on top. *You can prepare ahead up to this point.*

To reheat the cassoulet: Cook it in a moderately hot oven (190°C, Mark 5, 375°F) for $1\frac{1}{4}$–$1\frac{1}{2}$ hours or until very hot and browned. If the cassoulet is already warm, allow only $\frac{3}{4}$ hour for browning. Serve in the casserole.

Tomatoes Provençale

6–8 large tomatoes
50 g/2 oz/$\frac{1}{4}$ cup butter
2 cloves garlic, crushed
salt and freshly ground black pepper
50 g/2 oz/$\frac{1}{2}$ cup browned breadcrumbs

This recipe can easily be doubled or halved.

Cut the tomatoes in half, discarding the cores. Put them in a buttered baking dish. Melt the butter and add the garlic, salt and pepper. Sprinkle the breadcrumbs on the tomatoes and spoon the butter mixture on top. *You can prepare 12 hours ahead up to this point.*

A short time before serving, bake the tomatoes in a moderately hot oven (190°C, Mark 5, 375°F) for 12–15 minutes until just tender.

Escarole salad

2 heads escarole (Batavian endive)

For the dressing
2 tbs wine vinegar
$1\frac{1}{2}$ tsp Dijon mustard
salt and freshly ground black pepper
4 tbs olive oil
4 tbs double cream

You can make almost any quantity you
want of this salad.

Wash the escarole thoroughly: tear it into
bite-sized pieces and dry on a cloth or paper
towels. You can keep it in a plastic bag in
the refrigerator for up to 24 hours.
   For the dressing: Whisk the vinegar with
the mustard and salt and pepper until well
mixed. Gradually beat in the oil so the
dressing emulsifies and thickens slightly,
then slowly whisk in the cream so the
dressing thickens further. *It can be made up
to 24 hours ahead.*
   Just before serving, whisk the dressing
until it re-emulsifies. Mix it thoroughly with
the salad and taste for seasoning.

Apple Tartes Tatin

French pie pastry made with $225\,g/\frac{1}{2}\,lb/1\frac{3}{4}$
   cups flour (see 114)
$450\,g/1\,lb/2$ cups sugar
$2.25\,kg/5\,lb$ (about 20) tart apples
$100\,g/\frac{1}{4}\,lb/\frac{1}{2}$ cup butter
$5\,dl/1\,pt/2$ cups double cream, whipped
   until it holds a soft peak, or $5\,dl/1\,pt/2$
   cups sour cream (for serving)

two 25-cm/10-inch heavy frying pans

This recipe can easily be halved; if you
double it, make the pastry in 2 batches for 4
tartes.

Make the pastry and chill it. Set the oven at
moderately hot (190°C, Mark 5, 375°F).
   For caramel: Have a large pan ready with
plenty of cold water. Heat $175\,g/6\,oz/\frac{3}{4}$ cup
of the sugar in one pan, stirring occasionally
until melted. Cook until a deep golden
caramel colour (pale caramel is tasteless);
take from the heat and immediately plunge
the base of the pan into the cold water to
stop the caramel from cooking. *However, it
may continue cooking a moment or two in the
pan, so you must allow for this since caramel
burns easily.* Repeat with $175\,g/6\,oz/\frac{3}{4}$ cup
more sugar in the other pan.
   Peel the apples; halve and core them and
cut in very thin slices. Arrange them in a
neat overlapping pattern in the bottom of
the pans. Arrange another layer of apples at
right angles on top. *This ensures the tarte
does not collapse when turned out.* Dot with
butter, sprinkle with sugar, and continue
until the remaining apples, sugar, and
butter are used and both pans are very full.
   Divide the pastry in half, roll out each

half to a circle and cover the apples, trimming the edge neatly. Chill 15 minutes.

Bake the tartes in the heated oven for 30–35 minutes or until the apples are tender when tested with a knife and the pastry is lightly browned. Let the tartes cool in the pans. *You can prepare 6–8 hours ahead up to this point.*

A short time before serving, warm the tartes in a low oven or over a low heat on top of the stove until they are tepid. Turn out on a serving dish so the caramelized side is up. Serve slightly warm, with whipped cream or sour cream separately.

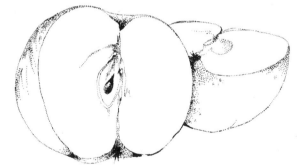

French Pie Pastry

225 g / ½ lb / 1¾ cups flour
pinch of salt
100 g / ¼ lb / ½ cup butter, softened
100 g / ¼ lb / ½ cup sugar
4 egg yolks
1 tsp vanilla extract

Sift the flour with the salt onto a marble slab or board and make a large well in the centre. Put the butter, sugar, egg yolks, and vanilla extract in the well and work them with the fingertips of one hand until the mixture is smooth. Using the whole hand, gradually work in the flour with the fingers and the heel of the hand in a rocking motion. Knead the dough lightly until smooth and chill it for 30 minutes. It can be kept, tightly covered, in the refrigerator for up to 48 hours.

An Elegant Lunch

Mushroom Tartlets

Chicken en Cocotte with Parma Ham

Duchesse Potatoes

Sautéed Cucumber

Petits Pots de Crème

Little details make this menu special. The savoury mushroom mixture is baked in individual tartlets instead of one large pie. The piped border of golden-brown duchesse potatoes which surrounds the entrée of baked chicken is a decorative touch, beloved by chefs. And not one but three flavours are to be found in the dessert custard pots.

The filling for mushroom tartlets is based on duxelles. This mushroom purée is flavoured with onion, parsley, and sometimes with garlic. It is named after the Marquis d'Uxelles, patron of the famous seventeenth-century chef, La Varenne. In this recipe the duxelles purée is enriched with egg yolks and cream and lightened with egg whites so that the tartlets become,

in effect, tiny soufflés. Like all soufflés, they should be served at once.

Chicken en cocotte with Parma ham could not be easier. The birds are browned in butter, then cooked in a covered casserole so they need no attention during cooking. The casserole method is a good alternative to roasting because the chicken cannot dry out. Parma ham adds an agreeably smoky flavour, but if this ham isn't available, you could substitute cubed or diced raw smoked bacon or ham or a vegetable such as onion, celery, courgettes, or tomatoes; they should be added towards the end of the cooking.

A simple piped border of duchesse potatoes is suggested here; the potato purée, stiffened with egg yolks, can also be piped in such designs as rosettes and figures of eight on a baking sheet, then browned in the oven. And if you feel you haven't got the design just right, simply pile the purée back in the icing bag and try again.

When it comes to pots de crème, you will find that the porcelain manufacturers have done half the work for you, letting their imagination run riot with irresistible sets of little heatproof mousse pots with lids, some with handles, some without, some plain, some decorated with flowers, fruits, and birds. As their name implies, they are equally suitable for chocolate or any other flavour of mousse, as well as the egg custard mixture used for pots de crème.

COUNTDOWN

1–2 Days Before
Make tartlet shells and keep in an airtight container.
Cook chicken, carve, and leave in casserole for reheating.
Make petits pots de crème.

Day Before
Make mushroom filling for tartlets, but do not add egg whites; keep tightly covered.
Parboil cucumbers and keep tightly covered.

1–2 Hours Before Serving
Pipe duchesse potatoes onto dishes or a baking sheet and brush with glaze.

30 Minutes Before Serving
Set oven at hot (200°C, Mark 6, 400°F).
Take pots de crème out of refrigerator.

20 Minutes Before Serving
Put potatoes in oven to brown.
Reheat chicken gently on top of stove.
Heat mushroom mixture, whip egg whites. and fill tartlets.

10 Minutes Before Serving
Take out potatoes; bake mushroom tartlets.
Transfer potatoes to a dish if on a baking sheet.

Just Before Serving Tartlets
Turn oven to low and keep chicken and potatoes warm.
Leave cucumbers to sauté over low heat.

After Serving Tartlets
Arrange chicken on platters, spoon over sauce and add watercress if used.
Transfer cucumbers to a serving dish.

Mushroom Tartlets

pie pastry made with 225 g/½ lb/1½ cups flour (page 51)

For filling
2 tbs butter
1 onion, finely chopped
350 g/¾ lb mushrooms, finely chopped
1 tbs chopped parsley
salt and freshly ground black pepper
4 eggs, separated
2.5 dl/½ pt/1 cup double cream
2 egg whites

10 deep tartlet pans (9–10 cm/3½–4 inches diameter); 12–13 cm/4½–5 inch plain or fluted pastry cutter

You can double or halve this recipe.

Make the pastry and chill it for about 30 minutes. Set the oven at moderately hot (190°C, Mark 5, 375°F).
    Roll out the dough to ½ cm/¼ inch thickness and stamp out 10 rounds with a plain or fluted pastry cutter. Line the dough into the tartlet pans so it comes a little way above the edge of the pans, set on a baking sheet, and chill until firm.
    Line the dough with greaseproof paper or foil and fill with dry rice or dried beans to help the dough keep its shape in the oven. Set on a baking sheet and bake in the heated oven for 12–15 minutes until the pastry is lightly browned. Remove the paper and rice after about 8 minutes cooking, so the pastry dries, Let the pastry shells cool in the pans, then remove them and store in an airtight container.

For the filling: Melt the butter in a heavy-

Chicken en Cocotte with Parma Ham

3 chickens ($1\frac{1}{2}$–$1\frac{3}{4}$ kg/3–$3\frac{1}{2}$ lb each)
salt and freshly ground black pepper
6 tbs butter
225 g/$\frac{1}{2}$ lb Parma ham, chopped
1 tbs rosemary, crushed
3.25 dl/$\frac{3}{4}$ pt/$1\frac{1}{2}$ cups white wine
1–2 bunches watercress (for garnish) –
   optional

trussing needle and string

based pan and sauté the onion gently until soft but not brown. Add the chopped mushrooms and cook over high heat, stirring occasionally until all the moisture has evaporated and the mixture is dry. Take from the heat and add the parsley and salt and pepper. Stir in the egg yolks and cream and cook over low heat, stirring constantly until the mixture thickens slightly. *Do not boil or it will curdle.* Take at once from the heat, taste for seasoning, and cover tightly – the mixture should be highly seasoned to balance the egg whites added later. *You can prepare 24 hours ahead up to this point.*

A short time before serving, set the oven at hot (200°C, Mark 6, 400°F). Set the pastry shells on a baking sheet. Heat the mushroom mixture over low heat until the base of the pan is hot to the touch. Stiffly whip the 6 egg whites and stir a little into the hot mushroom mixture. Add this mixture to the remaining egg whites and fold together as lightly as possible. Spoon the mixture into the pastry shells and bake in the heated oven for 8–10 minutes until puffed and brown. Serve at once.

You can easily halve this recipe or make it in large quantities for a crowd since it reheats well.

Set oven at moderate (180°C, Mark 4, 350°F).

Season the chickens inside with salt and pepper and truss them. In a large casserole, melt the butter and brown the chickens on all sides. Set them on their backs, add the Parma ham, rosemary, white wine, and pepper; *if the ham is salty, no extra salt may be needed.*

Cover and cook in the heated oven for about 40–50 minutes or until no pink juice runs from the centre of the chickens when they are lifted. Carve each chicken into 4 pieces – 2 legs and 2 breasts with wings (page 209). *You can prepare 48 hours ahead up to this point.* Keep the chickens in the casserole in the refrigerator.

If you have prepared ahead, reheat the chicken pieces in the casserole in a moderate oven (180°C, Mark 4, 350°F) for 15–20 minutes or on top of the stove until very hot.

Meanwhile, brown duchesse potatoes (see page 118). If done on heatproof platters, the chicken can then be arranged in the centre of the dish with the sauce and garnish spooned on top. Otherwise, serve the chicken on separate platters with watercress for garnish.

Duchesse Potatoes

8–10 medium potatoes, peeled
about 2.50/$\frac{1}{2}$pt/1$\frac{1}{4}$ cups milk
100 g/$\frac{1}{4}$ lb/$\frac{1}{2}$ cup butter
salt and pepper
5 egg yolks
1 egg, beaten with $\frac{1}{2}$ tsp salt (for glaze)

icing bag and large star nozzle

You can easily make half quantity of this
recipe, but if you try to double it, the
potatoes are almost impossible to mash
and beat.

Cook the potatoes in boiling water for
15–20 minutes until tender when tested
with a knife. Drain, return to pan, and dry
over low heat for 1–2 minutes. Work
through a food mill or ricer and add the
milk, butter, salt and pepper, and beat them
over the heat until light and fluffy – *the heat
expands the starch grains in the potatoes.* Add
more milk, if necessary, to make a fairly stiff
mixture. Take from the heat, beat in the
egg yolks and let cool. *You can prepare 12
hours ahead up to this point, but be sure the
potatoes are fairly soft, so that they can still be
piped after chilling for 12 hours.* Keep them,
tightly covered, in the refrigerator.

   An hour or two before serving, put the
potatoes into an icing bag fitted with a
large star nozzle and pipe a border of
rosettes around 1 or 2 heatproof platters
or baking dishes. Alternatively, pipe the
potatoes in mounds or figures of eight on a
buttered baking sheet. Brush the potatoes
with beaten egg glaze. A short time before
serving, bake them in a hot oven (200°C,
Mark 6, 400°F) for 8–10 minutes until
browned.

Sautéed Cucumber

4 cucumbers
100 g/$\frac{1}{4}$ lb/$\frac{1}{2}$ cup butter
salt and pepper
2 tbs chopped mint, dill, or parsley

This recipe can be halved or doubled.

Peel the cucumbers, cut them in half
lengthwise, and scoop out the seeds with a
teaspoon. Cut each half lengthwise 2 or 3
times, then crosswise into 5-cm/2-inch
sticks. Parboil them in boiling salted water
for 5 minutes and drain. *You can prepare 12
hours ahead up to this point.* Keep the
cucumbers tightly covered.

   Just before serving, melt the butter, add
the cucumbers, and sauté 5 minutes or
until just tender. Add salt, pepper, and the
chopped mint, dill, or parsley and serve. *Do
not sauté the cucumber for too long or it will
become bitter.*

Petits Pots de Crème

3 squares (75 g/3 oz) semi-sweet chocolate
7.5 dl/3 pt double cream
1 vanilla pod, split lengthwise, or 1 tsp
  vanilla extract
6 eggs
6 egg yolks
4 tbs sugar
1 tbs instant coffee dissolved in 1 tsp hot
  water

12 mousse pots with lids

The very best pots de crème are made with egg yolks only, so if you want to be extravagant, substitute 12 egg yolks for the 6 whole eggs in this recipe (making a total of 18 yolks). The recipe can easily be halved, and the custards keep well for 1–2 days in the refrigerator. If you have no mousse pots, custard cups are a less elegant alternative; cover them with foil during baking.

Melt the chocolate on a heatproof plate over a pan of hot water and let cool. Set the oven at moderate (180°C, Mark 4, 350°F).

Bring the cream almost to the boil with the vanilla pod, if used; cover and leave in a warm place to infuse for 10–15 minutes. Do not add vanilla extract at this point. Beat the eggs and egg yolks with the sugar until light and slightly thickened. Stir in the hot cream and strain this custard mixture. (The vanilla pod can be washed and dried to use again.) If you use vanilla extract, add it now.

Transfer the vanilla custard to a jug, and pour about a third of it into four mousse pots. Stir the dissolved coffee into the remaining custard in the jug and pour about half of it into four more mousse pots. Stir the cool but still melted chocolate into the remaining custard and pour it into the remaining mousse pots. *Although this last custard combines vanilla, coffee, and chocolate, the chocolate flavour will be dominant.*

Cover the mousse pots with the lids or foil, set them in a roasting pan half filled with water (a bain marie), and bring to the boil on top of the stove. Transfer to the heated oven and cook for 15–20 minutes or until a knife inserted near the centre of the custards comes out clean. *Do not overcook or they will curdle.* Let cool and store, covered, in the refrigerator. Let the pots de crème come to room temperature before serving.

Dinner in a Hurry

Oyster Soup

Pork Tenderloin Cauchoise

Potato Cake

Hot Raspberry Soufflé with Iced Vanilla Custard Sauce

Oyster soup is a great treat, especially if you can get plentiful supplies of this once cheap seafood delicacy. The soup is made by briefly sautéing oysters in butter until their edges curl; milk, salt and pepper are added; the soup is brought to the boil and sprinkled with parsley to serve. You follow the same principle when making an oyster stew for a main dish, but use half milk, half cream, and double the quantity of oysters. Both soup and stew are remarkably simple and remarkably good.

Pork tenderloin is the same cut as a beef fillet, but of course it is much smaller, weighing 450–675 g/1–1½ pounds. It is so lean and tender that it is almost indistinguishable from veal and much less expen-

sive. Tenderloin of pork is available at most butchers but if you cannot find it, you can substitute veal scaloppine. If you are using veal, simmer it only 10–15 minutes in the sauce since it is so thinly sliced.

The potato cake is a simple version of Pommes Anna, using thin strips instead of slices of potato. The cake can be cooked ahead and reheated, but do not stop preparation halfway because if the potato strips are soaked in cold water they will lose the starch which is needed to knit them together. An omelette pan is best for making this dish, but any well-seasoned pan will do.

The hot raspberry soufflé is the closest thing to being foolproof and so is ideal for beginners. It is based on raspberry jam, and the only work involved is beating the egg whites to make a meringue. The resulting soufflé texture is firmer than most, so it can be made and left up to an hour before cooking without harm, and since it rises straight up in the oven there's no need for a paper collar around the dish. The iced vanilla custard not only provides a foil to the hot soufflé, but it uses up the egg yolks left from the meringue. The soufflé is complete in itself, so if you are rushed, you can save time by leaving out the vanilla custard sauce.

Kebab Barbecue. Glowing coals invite guests to make their own kebabs from an array of marinated shrimps, lamb and vegetables. Saffron rice pilaf is the time-honoured accompaniment, with orange and almond tart as dessert

COUNTDOWN

Day Before or in the Morning
Brown pork, make sauce, cover, and cook
   in oven.
Make garnish for pork and let cool.
Make potato cake and cook.
Prepare ingredients and dish for soufflé.
Make vanilla custard sauce and chill.

45 Minutes Before Serving
Set oven at moderate (180°C, Mark 4,
   350°F).
Sauté oysters and leave in pan.

30 Minutes Before Serving
Put pork in oven to reheat.
Make raspberry soufflé and chill.
Reheat potato cake on top of stove.

15 Minutes Before Serving
Finish soup and keep warm.
Slice pork, replace in sauce, and keep
   warm; put garnish in oven to reheat.

After Serving Soup
Arrange pork and garnish on dish and
   serve.

15 Minutes Before Serving Dessert
Bake soufflé.

A Formal Buffet. Cooking for fifty is quite an
undertaking. Suggestions shown here include
beef in aspic, flanked by colourful vegetables and
served with a salad of new potatoes. Chocolate
snowball and a traditional trifle complete the
menu

Oyster Soup

1 kg/2 lb/1 qt standard shelled oysters, with
   their liquor
6 tbs butter
7.5 dl/3 pt milk
salt and freshly ground black pepper
2.5 dl/$\frac{1}{2}$ pt/1 cup double cream
2 tbs chopped parsley
oyster crackers for serving (optional)

This recipe can easily be halved or doubled.
If possible, make it at the last minute
because oysters tend to be tough when
reheated.

Drain the oysters, reserving their liquor. In
a large pan, melt the butter and sauté the
oysters over high heat for 1 minute or until
the edges curl. *Do not overcook or they will
be tough.* Add the milk with the oyster liquor
and plenty of salt and pepper and bring to
the boil. Add the cream, reheat until almost
boiling, and stir in the parsley. Taste for
seasoning and serve at once. Serve French
bread separately, if you like.

Pork Tenderloin Cauchoise

1 tbs oil
2 tbs butter
3–4 pork tenderloins (about $1\frac{3}{4}$ kg/4 lb)
2 onions, chopped
2 tbs flour
5–6 dl/1–$1\frac{1}{2}$ pt/2–$2\frac{1}{2}$ cups chicken or beef
   stock
2.5 dl/$\frac{1}{2}$ pt/1 cup white wine
2 shallots, chopped (optional)
1 clove garlic, crushed
bouquet garni
salt and freshly ground black pepper

For garnish
50 g/2 oz/$\frac{1}{4}$ cup butter
1 small head celery, sliced (about
   450 g/1 lb/4 cups)
salt and freshly ground black pepper
450 g/1 lb mushrooms, stems trimmed level
   with the caps and thickly sliced
50 g/2 oz/1 cup walnut halves
2 tbs chopped parsley

You can easily halve this recipe; it reheats
well and can be cooked in the oven or on
top of the stove.

If you use the oven, set it at moderate
(180°C, Mark 4, 350°F).

In a shallow casserole, heat the oil and
butter and brown the tenderloins on all
sides. Take out, add the onions, and cook
until soft but not brown. Add the flour and
cook, stirring, until browned. At once add
5 dl/1 pt/2 cups of the stock, with the white
wine, shallots if used, garlic, bouquet garni,
and seasoning, and replace the tenderloins.
Cover and simmer gently on top of the
stove or cook in the heated oven for $1\frac{1}{2}$–$1\frac{3}{4}$
hours or until the meat is very tender, add-
ing more stock if the mixture gets dry. Take
out the tenderloins, cut them in 1-cm/
$\frac{3}{8}$-inch diagonal slices, and return them to
the sauce.

For the garnish: Melt the butter in a heavy-
based pan, add the celery with salt and
pepper, and press a piece of foil on top.
Cover with the lid and cook very gently on
top of the stove for about 10 minutes or
until the celery is almost tender, stirring
occasionally. Add the mushrooms and continue cooking, uncovered, until tender. Add
the walnuts and taste for seasoning. *You
can prepare 24 hours ahead up to this point.*
Keep the pork and garnish separately in the
refrigerator.

If necessary, reheat the pork and garnish
over low heat on top of the stove a short
time before serving. Arrange the pork slices
overlapping down one side of a dish
Skim any fat from the sauce, taste for
seasoning, and spoon a little over the pork.
Spoon the garnish down the other side of
the dish. Sprinkle the garnish with
parsley, reheat the remaining sauce, and
serve it separately.

Potato Cake

2.25 kg/5 lb large potatoes, peeled
225 g/½ lb/1 cup butter
salt and pepper

two 18–21-cm/7–8-inch frying pans

This recipe can be halved or doubled, but do not try to make a potato cake larger than 18–21 cm/7–8 inches because it is hard to turn out. The cakes can be made ahead and reheated on top of the stove.

Cut peeled potatoes into strips about ½ cm/¼ inch wide and 5 cm/2 inches long; dry them thoroughly on paper towels. Spread 100 g/¼ lb/½ cup butter over the base and sides of each pan and press in a layer of potato strips. When a thick layer covers the base of the pan, sprinkle with salt and pepper. *The salt makes them stick together.* Add remaining potatoes, seasoning each layer, and mound them well. Cover both pans with buttered foil, tucking down the sides to keep the steam from escaping, and place a heatproof plate or pan lid with a weight on top.

    Cook the potatoes on top of the stove for 10 minutes or until the bottom is browned. To check the bottom, lift up one side with a metal spatula – the smell of browned butter is unmistakable. Transfer the pans to a moderately hot oven (190°C, Mark 5, 375°F) and bake for 30 minutes or until the potatoes are very tender. *You can prepare 24 hours ahead up to this point.* Keep the cake, covered, in the refrigerator.

    If necessary, reheat potatoes on top of the stove over low heat until very hot. Loosen the base of the potato cake with a metal spatula and turn it out onto a dish.

Hot Raspberry Soufflé

175 g/6 oz/¾ cup sugar
2 jars (350 g/¾ lb each) raspberry jam
juice 1 lemon
12 egg whites

two soufflé dishes (1½ l/3 pt capacity each)

This recipe can be halved easily, but do not try to double it because more egg whites are difficult to beat.

Set the oven at hot (200°C, Mark 6, 400°F). Thoroughly butter the soufflé dishes and sprinkle them with sugar, discarding the excess.
  Melt the jam with the lemon juice over low heat; work it through a strainer to remove the seeds and return the jam to the pan. Keep it in a warm place – *the base of the pan should be hot to the touch, but not burning.*
  Stiffly whip the egg whites and stir in the sugar with a large metal spoon until this meringue is glossy and forms tall peaks when the spoon is lifted. Add about a quarter to the warm jam and fold together thoroughly. *The jam will cook the meringue slightly and make it firm.* Add this mixture to the remaining egg whites and fold them together as lightly as possible. Spoon the mixture into the soufflé dishes and level the tops – they should be full to the brim. *You can prepare an hour ahead up to this point.* Keep the soufflés in the refrigerator.
  Bake the soufflés in the heated oven for 15–18 minutes or until puffed and brown. Serve at once, with iced vanilla custard sauce if you like.

Iced Vanilla Custard Sauce

7.5 dl/½ pt/3 cups milk
1 vanilla pod, split lengthwise, or 1 tsp vanilla extract
9 egg yolks
175 g/6 oz/¾ cup sugar
little sugar (for sprinkling)

You can make this custard ahead if you keep it tightly covered; the recipe can be halved or doubled. Some cooks like to make custard in a double boiler to insure that it will not get too hot and curdle.

Bring the milk almost to the boil with the vanilla pod and leave in a warm place to infuse for 10–15 minutes. Do not add vanilla extract at this point. Beat the egg yolks with 175 g/6 oz/¾ cup sugar until thick and light. Stir in half the hot milk and stir this mixture back into the remaining milk. Heat gently, stirring constantly, until the custard thickens slightly; if you draw your finger across the back of the spoon, it will leave a clear trail. *Do not overcook or boil the custard or it will curdle.*
  Take the custard at once from the heat and strain it into a bowl (the vanilla pod can be washed, dried, and used again). If you are using vanilla extract, add it now. Sprinkle lightly with sugar to prevent a skin from forming, cover tightly and chill.

MENUS
FOR
TWELVE

A Fork Lunch

A Winter Dinner

A Summer Dinner

Make-It-in-the-Morning Brunch

MENUS FOR TWELVE

People and things seem to come in twelves – the apostles, jurors, tribes of Israel, zodiac signs, and bottles of wine. A party for twelve also seems a natural event, but it will require organization. It's not so much the sheer mechanics of slicing vegetables or carving birds. It's also a matter of finding space to store partly prepared dishes. It means finding attractive platters and marshalling the requisite silverware and linen and glasses both for the table and for cocktails. As for cleaning up afterwards, a prime rule is to rinse items as they come from the table. This helps greatly with the later chores.

The Fork Lunch could not be simpler in organization or more satisfying to the eye. Two dishes from Italy – an antipasto platter of mixed hors d'oeuvre followed by a baked lasagne – are both easy to serve. The colourful iced dessert for this buffet meal – caramel nut parfait topped with whipped cream – is also Italian in inspiration.

If the occasion calls for a formal dinner, choose between these two seasonal menus. The Winter Dinner, featuring veal Orloff made with ham and mushroom purée, is easy to serve for large numbers, either buffet-style or seated at the table. A perfect cold-weather appetizer is the rich chestnut soup, garnished with spring onion.

Iced cucumber soup makes a refreshing start to a superb Summer Dinner of baby pigeon with green grapes, flanked by a salad of watercress. This luxury menu invites champagne or at least a good white wine like Pouilly Fumé or Meursault. Both summer and winter menus, by the way, are carefully designed so almost all cooking can be done ahead of time. For a more modest, country-style dinner, try the Square Meal suggested in Menus for Four. The entrée of beef roulades can easily be expanded to serve twelve, and this menu, too, can be made in advance.

Entertaining so many people at short notice is not easy,

but a Make-It-in-the-Morning Brunch of kedgeree (rice with salmon or smoked haddock and hard-boiled eggs) followed by baked apples will take a couple of hours from start to finish and still leave you time in between to set the table, arrange the flowers, and mix some drinks to welcome your guests.

Another morning-made meal is the Hearty Breakfast in Menus for Eight. Increase the number of grilled kidneys in bacon by half, and for the baked eggs Basquaise, simply add an extra onion and a green pepper to the vegetable mixture and use a couple of dozen eggs.

Outdoor meals for twelve can be adapted from the Outdoor Lunch of gazpacho, paella, and flan (caramel custard) and the Kebab Barbecue, both in Menus for Twenty-four, which are easy to cut in half.

A Fork Lunch

Antipasto Platter
Lasagne
Green Salad
Caramel Nut Parfait

The colour and charm of Italy is often echoed in the cooking, and nothing evokes better the contrasting aromas of its markets than the antipasti which traditionally begin a meal. Served on one big platter before (*ante*) the main course, these appetizers commonly include cold meats and fish, olives, anchovies, and pickled vegetables. If you have an Italian delicatessen, you will be able to find such delicacies as lonza (cured fillet of pork), bondiola (salami made with wine), and fresh mozzarella cheese. Most good grocery stores and supermarkets sell Parma ham and several varieties of sausage, and the tinned goods shelves will yield tuna, anchovies, sardines, peppers, and pimentos. In the following platter a broad selection of commonly available antipasti is suggested, along with a recipe for stuffed aubergine to make at home.

Lasagne needs no introduction as the perfect dish for informal parties. It is easy to serve and can be made in advance (indeed the flavour improves on standing) or frozen for a future occasion. Unless you are a pasta expert, don't bother to make your own. When layered with homemade meat sauce and béchamel flavoured with cheese, few pasta lovers can detect the difference. Serve the lasagne with a simple green salad tossed with vinaigrette dressing made with olive oil (page 41).

Experts agree that the best ice cream is made in a churn freezer. Parfaits, however, avoid all this bother, since the mixture is so rich that it can be frozen directly in the freezer without stirring. This particular parfait is flavoured with caramel and pecans or walnuts, a delectable variation of the caramel and almond mixture called praline.

Traditionally parfaits are frozen and served in parfait glasses. Any heavy, stemmed glasses will do, but don't risk your best crystal in the freezer. Parfaits also look pretty served in a soufflé dish and topped with strawberries and cream. If you tie a collar around the soufflé dish so the mixture comes above the edge when frozen, the parfait looks as though it has risen.

COUNTDOWN

1–2 Weeks Before
Make caramel nut parfait and freeze.

1–2 Days Before
Make stuffed aubergines for antipasto
platter.
Make meat and cheese sauce; cook
lasagne, layer with sauces, and keep
covered.

Day Before
Wash lettuce for salad and keep in plastic bag; make dressing.

In the Morning
Arrange all ingredients for antipasto
platter in dishes and keep covered.

1¼ Hours Before Serving
Set oven at moderate (180°C, Mark 4,
350°F).

1 Hour Before Serving
Bake lasagne in heated oven.

40 Minutes Before Serving
Whip cream for parfait decoration, put in
icing bag, and keep in refrigerator; hull
strawberries, if used.

20 Minutes Before Serving
Decorate parfaits and keep in refrigerator.

10 Minutes Before Serving
Transfer antipasto dishes to table.
Toss salad.
Turn oven to low to keep lasagne warm.

Antipasto Platter

225 g/½ lb Parma ham
225 g/½ lb salami
225 g/½ lb Mortadella sausage
100 g/¼ lb sardines in oil, drained
50 g/2 oz anchovy fillets, drained
200 g/7 oz tuna in oil, drained and flaked
525 g/17 oz mixed pickled vegetables,
  drained
225 g/½ lb black olives
225 g/½ lb green olives

For stuffed aubergines
7 baby aubergines or 3 medium aubergines
1.25 dl/¼ pt/½ cup olive oil
1 onion, chopped
2 tbs butter
4 tomatoes, peeled, seeded, and chopped
  (page 207)
2 cloves garlic, crushed
3 tbs chopped parsley
50 g/2 oz/½ cup fresh white breadcrumbs
salt and freshly ground black pepper
3 tbs grated Parmesan cheese (for
  sprinkling)
By changing quantities and adding or sub-
tracting ingredients you can easily adapt
this recipe for more or fewer people.

For the stuffed aubergines: Set the oven at
moderate (180°C, Mark 4, 350°F). Slice the
aubergines in half lengthwise, score deeply
on the cut side, sprinkle with salt, and leave
30 minutes to draw out the bitter juices.
Rinse with cold water and dry on paper
towels. Heat the oil in a large pan and
sauté the aubergine halves gently, cut side
down, until browned. Transfer to the heated
oven and cook until tender, allowing 5–10
minutes for the baby aubergines or 15
minutes for the medium ones. Scoop out the

flesh and chop it, reserving the shells.

Sauté the onion in the butter until soft and mix it with the chopped aubergines, tomatoes, garlic, parsley, breadcrumbs, and salt and pepper to taste. Stuff the aubergine shells with the mixture, mounding it well, and sprinkle with the cheese. Arrange them in a buttered baking dish and bake in the heated oven for 15–20 minutes or until lightly browned. Let the aubergines cool and keep covered in refrigerator. *They can be cooked up to 48 hours ahead.* To serve, cut each medium aubergine in quarters, but leave baby aubergine halves in one piece.

Arrange all the ingredients in separate dishes, if possible matching ones, and set on a large tray. This can be done 3–4 hours in advance if the dishes are kept, covered with plastic wrap, in the refrigerator.

Lasagne

1.2 kg/1½ lb lasagne
50 g/2 oz/¾ cup grated Parmesan cheese (for sprinkling)

For the meat sauce
4 onions, chopped
4 tbs oil
1 kg/2 lb minced beef
1 kg/2 lb minced pork
2 tins (175 g/6 oz each) tomato paste
3 cloves garlic, crushed
bouquet garni
5–6 dl/1–1¼ pt/2–2½ cups stock
5 dl/1 pt/2 cups red wine
pinch of ground nutmeg
1 tsp ground allspice
salt and freshly ground black pepper

For the cheese sauce
100 g/¼ lb/½ cup butter
50 g/2 oz/½ cup flour
1½ l/2¼ pt/6 cups milk
salt and freshly ground black pepper
pinch of nutmeg
3 egg yolks (optional)
75 g/3 oz/1 cup grated Parmesan cheese

This recipe can easily be halved; if you double it, you will need to layer it in several baking dishes or, at a pinch, in a roasting pan.

For the meat sauce: In a heavy-based saucepan sauté the onions in the oil until soft but not brown. Add the beef and pork and cook, stirring, until lightly browned. Add the tomato paste, garlic, bouquet garni, 5 dl/1 pt of the stock, red wine, nutmeg, allspice, salt and pepper, and bring to the boil. Simmer, uncovered, for 45–50 minutes, stirring occasionally, until the sauce is thick and dark in colour. Add more stock during cooking if the sauce gets very thick and sticks to the pan, Discard the bouquet garni and taste for seasoning.

Meanwhile bring a roasting pan of salted water to the boil. Add half the lasagne and simmer, stirring occasionally to prevent sticking, for 12 minutes or until almost tender but still firm to the teeth (*al dente*). Transfer to a colander with a slotted spoon, rinse with hot water to wash away the starch, and keep the lasagne in a bowl with a 10-cm/4-inch covering of warm water to prevent them from sticking together. Cook the remaining lasagne in the same way.

For the cheese sauce: In a saucepan melt the butter, stir in the flour, and when they are foaming, pour in the milk. Bring to the boil, stirring constantly, add salt, pepper, and nutmeg, and simmer 2 minutes. Take from the heat and beat in the egg yolks, if used, to enrich the sauce, followed by the Parmesan cheese. *Do not reheat the sauce or the cheese will cook into strings.*

To assemble the lasagne: Spoon a layer of meat sauce in the bottom of 2 or 3 baking dishes. Drain several lengths of lasagne on paper towels and lay them on the meat sauce. Add a layer of cheese sauce, followed by another layer of drained lasagne, and continue adding layers until the dishes are full and all the ingredients are used, ending with a generous layer of cheese sauce. Sprinkle the top with the 50 g/2 oz/$\frac{3}{4}$ cup grated cheese. *You can prepare 48 hours ahead up to this point.* Keep the lasagne, covered, in the refrigerator.

To serve: Bake the lasagne in a moderate oven (180°C, Mark 4, 350°F) for 1 hour or until it is bubbling and browned.

Caramel Nut Parfait

675 g/1½ lb/3 cups sugar
225 g/½ lb/2 cups coarsely chopped pecans
   or walnuts
7.5 dl/½ pt/3 cups double cream, whipped
   until it holds a soft peak

For meringue
350 g/¾ lb/1½ cups sugar
2.5 dl/½ pt/1 cup water
8 egg whites

For decoration
1.8 dl/6 fl. oz/¾ cup double cream, stiffly
   whipped
12 whole strawberries or 12 walnut or
   pecan halves

*12 parfait or stemmed glasses or 2 soufflé
dishes (1 1/2 pt capacity each), icing bag and
medum star nozzle*

In this recipe the meringue and cream must
be whipped in 2 batches because such a
large quantity will overflow from a normal-
sized mixer. However, the caramel nut
flavouring can be made at one time. Quantities can easily be halved to serve six. If
you double the recipe, it must be made
twice.

Oil a baking sheet. Put the 675 g/1½ lb/3
cups sugar in a heavy pan and heat gently,
stirring occasionally, until the sugar melts
and has started to caramelize. Stir in the
walnut or pecans and cook the mixture,
stirring, to a rich golden brown caramel.
Immediately pour the mixture onto the
baking sheet and leave until cold and hard.
Tie the caramel in a heavy cloth and pound
with a mallet or rolling pin so it breaks up
into fairly coarse granules.

For the meringue: Heat 175 g/6 oz/¾ cup of
the sugar with 1.25 dl/¼ pt/½ cup water
until dissolved; bring to the boil and boil
without stirring until the syrup forms a
thread between finger and thumb when a
little is lifted on a spoon. Meanwhile stiffly
whip 4 egg whites. Beat in the boiling sugar
syrup in a steady stream and continue beating until the meringue is cool and very
thick. Fold in half the crushed caramel mixture, followed by 3.25 dl/¾ pt/1½ cups cream,
lightly whipped.

Spoon the mixture into 6 parfait or
stemmed glasses; cover it and freeze. Alternatively, if you use a soufflé dish, tie a
collar of greaseproof paper or foil so it ex-
tends 5–8 cm/2–3 inches above the edge of
the dish. Pour in the parfait mixture – it
will come 2–5 cm/1–2 inches above the
edge of the dish – cover and freeze. Make
the remaining parfait in the same way.

A short time before serving, decorate the
parfaits with rosettes of whipped cream,
using an icing bag and medium star nozzle.
Top each rosette with a strawberry or a
walnut or pecan half. If you use a soufflé
dish, remove the collar. If parfaits were
made more than 12 hours ahead, let them
soften in the refrigerator for about 1 hour
before serving.

A Winter Dinner

Chestnut Soup
Veal Orloff
Leaf Spinach
Savarin with Pineapple

Unlike so much produce, which is available year-round, chestnuts remain a winter speciality. Rich and smooth, with an elusive hint of smoke, chestnut soup is the ideal opening to dinner on a cold night. Fresh chestnuts are tedious to peel, and there is no substitute for patience as you strip off the skins, one by one, after softening them in hot water. If you feel you have to cheat and use canned chestnuts packed in water, you must expect to pay the price in money and flavour. (Four 275 g/10 oz tins will be the equivalent of the fresh chestnuts.) A garnish of chopped spring onion adds a refreshing touch of colour to the soup, or if you prefer, you can use chopped celery tops, chives, or fried croûtons.

The Orloffs were among the many noble Russian families who lent their names to the creations of French chefs. This particular dish consists of roast veal that is sliced, sandwiched with ham and a mushroom (or sometimes onion) purée, and then coated with cheese sauce, It is one of the few roast meat recipes that can be completely prepared ahead and reheated, and thus is invaluable for formal dinners. The sharpness of the accompanying leaf spinach is an excellent foil for the richness of the mushroom purée and cheese sauce.

The connection between Jean Anthelme Brillat-Savarin, the nineteenth-century French gastronome, and the rum-soaked coffee cake named after him would seem to be as tenuous as that between the Orloffs and veal. However, the epicure would certainly have appreciated the tribute to his name, though no inference is to be drawn about his fondness for spirits. A savarin is a yeast cake which, when still warm, is basted with hot rum-flavoured sugar syrup until it is saturated and swells to almost twice its original size. The cake is always baked in a plain ring mould (a savarin mould), and in this recipe, slices of fresh pineapple are inserted between slices of the cake in a classic presentation known as a turban. Don't be tempted to use tinned pineapple when fresh is not available, but instead fill the centre of the cake with fresh strawberries.

COUNTDOWN

1–2 Weeks Ahead
Make savarins and freeze.

2 Days Ahead
Make chestnut soup.
Pot roast veal and chill.

Day Before
Make duxelles purée, slice veal, and
    assemble on platters. Coat with sauce,
    let cool, and cover with plastic wrap.
Take savarin from freezer and leave to
    thaw; make apricot glaze.

In the Morning
Chop spring onion for soup garnish and
    keep covered.
Wash fresh spinach and keep in plastic
    bag.
Prepare pineapple and keep covered.

3–4 Hours Before Serving
Cook fresh or frozen spinach and drain.
Soak savarins with syrup, arrange on
    serving dish with pineapple, and coat
    with glaze. Cover and keep at room
    temperature.

45 Minutes Before Serving
Set oven at moderate (180°C, Mark 4,
    350°F).

30 Minutes Before Serving
Reheat veal Orloff in oven.

10 Minutes Before Serving
Add cream to soup and reheat.
Reheat spinach in butter and transfer to
    serving dish.

Just Before Serving
Turn oven to low and keep spinach and
    veal Orloff warm.

A Winter Dinner

Chestnut Soup

1½ kg/3 lb fresh chestnuts
100 g/¼ lb/½ cup butter
2 onions, chopped
6 stalks celery, chopped
1 clove garlic, crushed
1½ l/3 pt/6 cups chicken stock
salt and pepper
5 dl/1 pt/2 cups single cream
6 spring onions very thinly sliced (for
garnish)

You can halve this recipe, or if you have an
outsize pan, you can double it.

To peel the chestnuts: Pierce each one with a
pointed knife. Put them in a pan with water
to cover and bring just to the boil. Lift out a
few at a time, and while they are still
warm, peel off the outer and inner skin. *If
the chestnuts become hard to peel as they cool,
reheat them but do not boil for more than 1
minute.* Coarsely chop them.

   In a large pan, melt the butter and sauté
the chestnuts until lightly browned. Add the
onion and celery and continue cooking over
low heat until all the butter is absorbed and
the vegetables are soft. Add the garlic,
stock, and salt and pepper, cover and
simmer 30–40 minutes until the chestnuts
are very tender. Purée the soup in a blender
or work it through a food mill. *You can
prepare 48 hours ahead up to this point.* Keep
soup covered in the refrigerator.

   Just before serving, reheat the soup, add
the cream, and taste for seasoning. Spoon
into bowls and sprinkle each bowl with a
little chopped spring onion.

Veal Orloff

2 tbs oil
2 tbs butter
2–3 kg/5–6 lb boneless veal roast, barded,
    rolled, and tied (page 210)
1 onion, chopped
1 carrot, chopped
5 dl/1 pt/1–2 cups chicken or beef stock
2.5 dl/$\frac{1}{2}$ pt/1 cup white wine
bouquet garni
salt and freshly ground black pepper
12–14 thin slices cooked ham
5 tbs grated Parmesan cheese

For the duxelles
50 g/2 oz/$\frac{1}{4}$ cup butter
1 onion, finely chopped
675 g/1$\frac{1}{2}$ lb mushrooms, finely chopped
1 clove garlic, crushed
2 shallots, finely chopped
2 tbs chopped parsley

For the cheese sauce
175 g/6 oz/$\frac{3}{4}$ cup butter
75 g/3 oz/$\frac{3}{4}$ cup flour
2 1/4 pt milk
3 egg yolks
1 tsp Dijon mustard
50 g/2 oz/$\frac{3}{4}$ cup grated Parmesan cheese

This recipe can easily be halved. It is also perfectly possible to make veal Orloff for a grand dinner for 24 by using 2 veal roasts.

To pot roast the meat: Set the oven at moderate (180°C, Mark 4, 350°F). In a large casserole or a roasting pan, heat the oil and butter and brown the veal on all sides. Take it out, add the onion and carrot and cook gently until soft but not brown. Replace the veal, add 2.5 dl/$\frac{1}{2}$ pt/1 cup of stock, the wine, bouquet garni, salt and pepper. Cover with the lid or with foil if using a roasting pan. Roast the veal in the heated oven allowing 30 minutes per pound (450 g) or until tender when pierced with a skewer. Baste the meat occasionally and add more stock if the liquid in the pan evaporates. Let the veal cool to tepid in the pan, take out and chill it. Strain the cooking liquid and chill also.

For the duxelles: Melt the butter in a heavy-based pan and sauté the onion gently until soft but not brown. Add the chopped mushrooms and cook over high heat, stirring occasionally, until all the moisture has evaporated. Add the garlic and shallot and continue cooking over low heat for 1 minute. Take from the heat and add the parsley and plenty of salt and pepper.

To assemble the dish: Discard the strings and barding fat from the veal and cut it in 7 mm/$\frac{3}{8}$-inch slices. On one or two heat-proof platters reassemble the slices, sandwiching every other slice with duxelles and the ones in between with ham. *Prop up the first slice with the leftover ends of the veal so that the meat sits up well like a sliced loaf.*

Leaf Spinach

For the cheese sauce: In a saucepan, melt the butter, stir in the flour, and when they are foaming, pour in 1½ l/3 pt/6 cups of the milk. Heat, stirring constantly, until the sauce thickens and simmer 2 minutes. Take from the heat and beat in the egg yolks. Add the mustard with salt and pepper and stir in the cheese – the sauce will be quite thick. *Do not reheat the sauce or it will cook into strings.* Spoon about a third over the top of the meat to form a thick coating. Thin the remaining sauce by stirring in the remaining milk and spoon it over the meat and the surrounding platter. Sprinkle with the 5 tablespoons grated Parmesan cheese. *You can prepare 24 hours ahead up to this point.* Keep the veal, tightly covered, in the refrigerator.

   To serve: Bake the veal in a moderate oven (180°C, Mark 4, 350°F) for 25–30 minutes or until the sauce is bubbling and browned. Skim solidified fat from cooking liquid, reheat, taste for seasoning, and serve separately with the veal as gravy.

1¾ kg/4 lb fresh spinach or 6 packages
   frozen leaf spinach
100 g/¼ lb/½ cup butter
juice of ½ lemon
¼ tsp ground nutmeg
salt and freshly ground black pepper

This recipe can easily be halved or doubled.

If you use fresh spinach, discard the stems and wash the leaves in several changes of water. Put it in a large pan with 1 cm/ ½ inch of salted water and cook 5 minutes, stirring once or twice. Cook frozen spinach according to package directions. Drain the spinach thoroughly and press it in a colander with a plate to extract all the water. *You can prepare 3–4 hours ahead up to this point.*

   Just before serving, melt the butter in a large pan, add the spinach, lemon juice, nutmeg, and pepper, and cook, stirring, until it is very hot and all the butter is absorbed. Taste for seasoning before serving.

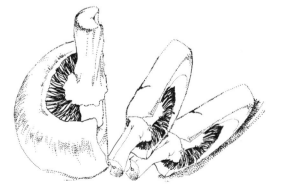

Savarin with Pineapple

2 medium pineapples, peeled and sliced
  (page 207)
50 g/2 oz/$\frac{1}{4}$ cup sugar, or to taste
2.5 dl/$\frac{1}{2}$ pt/1 cup apricot jam glaze
  (page 92)

For the savarins
450 g/1 lb/2$\frac{1}{2}$ cups flour
1 tsp salt
2 tbs sugar
6 tbs warm water
1$\frac{1}{2}$ packages dry yeast or 1$\frac{1}{2}$ cakes compressed yeast or 25 g/1 oz fresh yeast or
  12 g/$\frac{1}{2}$ oz dried yeast
5 eggs
1.25/$\frac{1}{4}$ lb/$\frac{3}{4}$ cup butter

For the syrup
450 g/1 lb/2 cups sugar
7.5 dl/1$\frac{1}{2}$ pt/3 cups water
pared rind and juice of 1 lemon
5 tbs rum

2 savarin or ring moulds (1$\frac{1}{2}$l/3 pt capacity each)

You can halve this recipe, but when you double it, the dough is difficult to work so you must make 2 batches. The savarin can be baked ahead and frozen.

For the savarins: Sift flour into a bowl with the salt and 2 tablespoons sugar. Make a well in the centre and pour in the warm water. Sprinkle or crumble the yeast over the water and let stand 5 minutes or until the yeast is dissolved. Add the eggs and stir with the hand, gradually drawing in the flour to form a smooth dough – it will be almost pourable. Beat for 5 minutes or until the dough is very elastic. Cover the bowl with a damp cloth and let stand in a warm

place for $\frac{3}{4}$–1 hour or until the dough has doubled in bulk. Brush the savarin moulds with melted butter, cool in the freezer for 5–10 minutes, and brush again, *This double coating of butter prevents the savarin from sticking.*

When the dough has risen, cream the butter and beat it into the dough a little at a time. Spoon into the prepared moulds and let stand again in a warm place for 25–30 minutes or until the dough reaches the top of the moulds. Set the oven at hot (200°C, Mark 6, 400°F).

Bake the savarins in the heated oven for 20–25 minutes or until they are browned and shrink from the sides of the pan. Turn out and let cool slightly. If you are prepar-ing ahead, let the savarins cool completely, wrap tightly, and store in an airtight con-tainer for up to 24 hours, or in the freezer.

Not more than 6 hours before serving, com-plete the savarins: Make sugar syrup by heat-ing the sugar with the water until dissolved, Bring to the boil, add pared lemon rind and simmer 5 minutes. Take from heat and add lemon juice and rum. If savarins were pre-pared ahead, heat them in a low oven (150°C, Mark 2, 300°F) for 5 minutes; set them on a rack over a tray to catch drip-pings of syrup. Baste the savarins with the hot syrup until all is absorbed, reheating the syrup that falls into the tray. The savarins will swell and look shiny; transfer them to dishes.

Prepare pineapple slices and sprinkle with sugar to taste. Cut each savarin diagonally in 6–8 pieces but do not separate them. Insert a slice of pineapple between each so the finished savarins look like turbans. Brush both the cakes and pineapple slices with melted apricot glaze. Cover with plastic wrap and keep at room temperature.

A Summer Dinner

Iced Cucumber Soup
Stuffed Pigeon Véronique
Watercress Salad
Peaches or Strawberries
Cardinal

Come summer, evey restaurant and every cook turns to that favourite soup, vichyssoise. This menu offers you a splendid variation by substituting cucumbers for leeks; otherwise the recipe remains the same, producing a refreshing soup whose flavour depends very much on using home-made chicken stock. When served hot, perhaps on a winter day, cucumber soup takes on quite a different character, reminiscent of courgettes, the cucumber's cousin.

Véronique is a classic garnish of green grapes in a wine sauce, and though usually associated with sole, its tartness suits the gamey flavour of pigeon to perfection. Try to get good, plump young birds, but cook older ones a little longer, till tender.

In this recipe the pigeon are stuffed with a pilaf made from buckwheat or from cracked wheat. Buckwheat, which is more like a flowering plant than a cereal (bees love its blossom), is better known as kasha, a staple in the diet of Central Europe. The French call it Saracen wheat, and indeed it may well have originated in the Middle East. Cracked wheat is what it sounds – whole wheat grains that are boiled, baked, and then cracked to varying degrees of coarseness. It too has another name – bulgur. You will find both these stuffings have a nutlike flavour with much more body than rice.

Watercress is invaluable as a garnish and as a salad green. Here both roles are combined; dressed simply with lemon juice, the watercress is arranged down one side of the platter of pigeon, making a one-dish main course that is easy to serve.

Peaches cardinal is one of those simple recipes which outshine many more elaborate creations. The origin of the name is not hard to find as the fruit is coated with a brilliant raspberry sauce of the same hue as a cardinal's robes. If you use the raspberry sauce on strawberries, the scarlet motif is carried to the ultimate. The recipe should be made several hours ahead so the fruit and sauce have time to blend.

COUNTDOWN

Day Before
Make cucumber soup and keep covered.
Make cracked wheat or buckwheat stuffing, fill pigeon and cook; leave in roasting pan ready for reheating.
Wash watercress and keep in plastic bag.
Make peaches or strawberries cardinal and keep tightly covered.

1 Hour Before Serving
Set oven at moderate (180°C, Mark 4, 350°F).
Whip cream if serving with fruit.
Chop chives for soup.
Take peaches or strawberries cardinal out of refrigerator.

40 Minutes Before Serving
Put pigeon in oven to reheat.

15 Minutes Before Serving
Transfer pigeon to serving dish, cover, turn oven to low, and keep warm.
Finish sauce for pigeon and keep warm; do not add grapes.
Spoon soup into bowls, add chives, and serve.

After Serving Soup
Add grapes to sauce, reheat, spoon over pigeon, and serve the rest separately.
Toss watercress with lemon juice and arrange round the pigeon.

Iced Cucumber Soup

4 cucumbers
6 tbs butter
2 medium potatoes, peeled and thinly sliced
2 1/4 pt chicken stock (page 210)
salt and freshly ground black pepper
5 dl/1 pt/2 cups double cream
4 tbs chopped chives (for garnish)

You can halve this recipe without trouble, but you will need a big pan if you double it.

Wipe the cucumbers, but do not peel them. Cut them lengthwise, scoop out the seeds with a teaspoon, and thinly slice the flesh.
   In a large pan, melt the butter, add the potatoes and cucumbers, and press a piece of foil on top. *Do not let the vegetables brown.* Add the stock, salt and pepper, cover and simmer 10–15 minutes. Purée the soup in a blender, return it to the pan, and add the cream. Bring just back to boil, take from the heat, taste for seasoning and strain, Cover and chill it. *You can prepare 24 hours ahead up to this point.*
   Just before serving, taste the soup for seasoning (cold mixtures often need more seasoning), spoon into bowls, and sprinkle each bowl with a few chopped chives.

Stuffed Pigeon Véronique

12 pigeon
175 g/6 oz/$\frac{3}{4}$ cup butter
salt and freshly ground black pepper

For the stuffing
450 g/1 lb (about 2 cups) coarse cracked
    wheat or buckwheat
1 egg, beaten to mix
1 1/2 pt/4 cups water
225 g/$\frac{1}{2}$ lb/1$\frac{1}{2}$ cups whole blanched almonds

For the sauce
5 dl/1 pt/2 cups white wine
5 dl/1 pt/2 cups chicken stock
1 tbs arrowroot mixed to a paste with 2 tbs
    water
450 g/1 lb (about 2$\frac{1}{2}$ cups) seedless green
    grapes
1.25 dl/$\frac{1}{4}$ pt/$\frac{1}{2}$ cup double cream

trussing needle and string

You can easily halve this recipe or double it
if you have two ovens for cooking the
pigeon. Cracked wheat and buckwheat are
available in Middle Eastern and health food
stores.

For the stuffing: Set the oven at moderate
(180°C, Mark 4, 350°F). Put the cracked
wheat or buckwheat in a heavy-based casserole, stir in the egg, and cook over high
heat, stirring constantly, for 8–10 minutes
until the grains of wheat are dry and separated. Add the water and salt and pepper,
cover and bring to the boil. Cook in the
heated oven allowing 25–30 minutes for the
cracked wheat or 10–15 minutes for the
buckwheat or until tender and all the water
is absorbed. Take out and let cool slightly.
Toast the almonds in the heated oven for
10–12 minutes until browned and stir them

into the cracked wheat or buckwheat; taste
for seasoning and let the stuffing cool. Turn
up the oven heat to moderately hot (190°C,
Mark 5, 375°F).

Fill the stuffing into the pigeon and truss
them (page 208). In a pan, melt half the
butter and brown half the pigeon on all
sides. Transfer them to a roasting pan and
brown the remaining pigeon in the remaining butter. Put all the birds in the roasting
pans, pour over the butter from the pan,
and sprinkle with salt and pepper. Cover the
birds tightly with foil and cook in the
heated oven for 60–65 minutes or until very
tender.

In a saucepan, boil the wine until reduced by half. Add the grapes, simmer 1
minute, lift them out with a slotted spoon
and reserve. When the pigeon are tender,
take them out and discard trussing strings.
Discard any fat from the pan, add the stock,
and heat, stirring to dissolve the pan juices.
Strain the mixture into the reduced wine.
*You can prepare 24 hours ahead up to this
point.* If you are preparing ahead, replace
the pigeon in the roasting pan, pour over
the wine and stock, and cover tightly with
foil. Keep in the refrigerator. Before making
sauce, reheat the pigeon in a moderate
oven (180°C, Mark 4, 350°F) for 20–25
minutes.

To make sauce: Bring the wine and stock to
the boil in a saucepan and whisk in the
arrowroot paste until the sauce thickens.
Add the grapes and cream, bring just back
to the boil, and taste for seasoning. Arrange
the pigeon down one side of a platter and
keep warm. Spoon a little of the sauce over
the pigeon and serve the rest separately.
Arrange watercress salad down the other
side of the platter.

Watercress Salad

5 medium bunches watercress
juice of 2 lemons

This recipe can be halved or doubled.

Wash the watercress thoroughly, discarding the thick stems. Dry it well in a salad basket or on paper towels; it can be kept in a plastic bag in the refrigerator for up to 24 hours. Just before serving, toss the watercress with the lemon juice.

Peaches or Strawberries Cardinal

16–18 ripe peaches or 5.2 kg/8 lb strawberries
3.25 dl/$\frac{3}{4}$ pt/1$\frac{1}{2}$ cups double cream, stiffly whipped – for serving (optional)

For the sauce
5 packages frozen raspberries
4 tbs kirsch
225–450 g/$\frac{1}{4}$–$\frac{1}{2}$ lb/$\frac{1}{2}$–1 cup icing sugar

You can easily halve or double this recipe. For an informal buffet, you may prefer to slice the peaches instead of leaving them in halves, so they are easier to eat. In this case let the dish stand only 2–3 hours instead of 6–12 hours before serving.

Halve, stone, and peel the peaches (see page 208). If you are using strawberries, hull them and wash only if they are very sandy. Pile the fruit in a glass bowl.

For the sauce: Purée the raspberries in a blender with the kirsch and sugar to taste – the sauce should be quite sweet to balance the tartness of the fruit. Strain to remove the seeds and pour over the fruit so it is completely coated. Cover and chill 6–12 hours. Let stand at room temperature 1–2 hours before serving. If you like, serve a bowl of whipped cream separately.

Make-It-In-the-Morning Brunch

Kedgeree
Tomato or Escarole Salad
Baked Apples
Screwdriver or Orange Juice

Brunch is a free and easy meal and you can make of it what you please. Perhaps you prefer a late and lavish breakfast with plenty of steaming hot coffee, fresh rolls, and eggs any style. Or, at the other end of the scale, you may favour a full-blown buffet, differing only in title from a regular lunch. In between these extremes lie traditional breakfast dishes like devilled kidneys, creamed chicken, and kedgeree.

Brunch is the ideal occasion to revive such recipes. Kedgeree dates from the time when the day's first meal was more than cereal and toast, and England ruled an empire. The original Indian dish, kitchri, was a robust mixture of rice and lentils laced with plenty of spice. To suit their palates, the British kept the rice base but toned down the spice to a light touch of curry. As a reminder of home, they added smoked haddock or salmon with hard-boiled eggs.

Any light salad is fine with kedgeree. Since tomatoes are one of India's favourite vegetables, the tomato salad (page 40) minus the watercress is appropriate, but escarole salad (page 113) or a simple green salad would go equally well. Don't forget to increase the quantities.

Baked apples are an excellent ending to the meal, or, if you like, you can reverse the order of the menu and serve the fruit first, as at breakfast. The recipe is simplicity itself, with a choice of dried fruit or chocolate filling for the apples.

The countdown for this menu is planned so all the cooking is done the morning of the brunch, but you may prefer to prepare the day before. The kedgeree can be made as far as the final mixing; the vegetables and dressing for the salad can be prepared and the apples baked. All you need do in the morning is reheat and mix the main dish, toss the salad, and warm the dessert.

The bracing flavour of the fresh orange juice, whether plain or mixed with vodka in a screwdriver, is the best accompaniment to this menu.

143

COUNTDOWN

2–3 Hours Before Serving

Set oven at moderate (180°C, Mark 4, 350°F).

Hard-boil eggs for kedgeree, drain and cover with cold water; chop parsley.

Add wine, water, and seasonings to salmon or milk to smoked haddock; cover and cook in oven.

Peel and slice tomatoes for salad or wash salad greens; make dressing.

Complete tomato salad, but do not add dressing to green salad.

1½–2½ Hours Before Serving

Take out smoked haddock and let cool.

Prepare apples for baking.

Boil rice.

1¼–2¼ Hours Before Serving

Take out salmon and let cool; turn oven heat to 190°C, Mark 5, 375°F.

Peel and chop hard-boiled eggs.

Drain rice and rinse with hot water.

1–2 Hours Before Serving

Flake salmon or haddock; cook curry powder in butter and add fish and eggs.

Spread rice in buttered dish.

Whip cream to serve with apples.

40 Minutes Before Serving

Bake apples.

15 Minutes Before Serving

Turn oven to moderate (180°C, Mark 4, 350°F) and put rice to reheat with apples.

Reheat fish mixture on top of stove.

Toss escarole or green salad with dressing.

5 Minutes Before Serving

Mix fish and rice together with cream and parsley.

Take out apples and let cool to warm.

Kedgeree

1.75 kg/4 lb piece fresh salmon or
   1.75 kg/4 lb smoked haddock fillet
750 g/1½ lb/3 cups rice
225 g/½ lb/1 cup butter
12 hard-boiled eggs, coarsely chopped
3.25 dl/¾ pt/1½ cups double cream
salt and pepper
6 tbs chopped parsley

For cooking salmon
2.5 dl/½ pt/1 cup white wine
2.5 dl/½ pt/1 cup water
6 peppercorns
few sprigs parsley

Or for cooking smoked haddock
5 dl/1 pt/2 cups milk

If you double this recipe, it is easier to do the final mixing in two casseroles; you can easily halve the quantities.

To cook the salmon: Set the oven at moderate (180°C, Mark 4, 350°F). Put the fish in a casserole, pour over the wine and water and add the peppercorns and parsley. Cover tightly, bring to the boil and poach in the heated oven for 25–30 minutes or until the fish just flakes easily when tested with a fork. Let cool in the cooking liquid.

To cook the smoked haddock: Set the oven at moderate (180°C, Mark 4, 350°F). Put the fish in a buttered baking dish, pour over the milk and cover with foil. Cook in the heated oven for 15–20 minutes or until the fish flakes easily. Let it cool.

Cook the rice in plenty of boiling salted water for 10–12 minutes or until just tender. Drain, rinse with hot water, and leave in a colander to drain for 10 minutes, poking drainage holes with the handle of a spoon. Spread the rice in a shallow buttered baking dish or roasting pan.

Drain salmon or smoked haddock and flake, discarding skin and bones. In a large, heavy-based casserole, melt the butter, add the curry powder and cook gently 2 minutes. Add the flaked fish and chopped eggs. *You can prepare 24 hours ahead up to this point.* Keep the fish mixture and rice, covered, in the refrigerator.

To serve: Heat the rice, uncovered, in a moderate oven (180°C, Mark 4, 350°F) for 10–15 minutes until hot and fluffy, stirring occasionally. Gently heat the fish mixture on top of the stove stirring occasionally. Add the rice to the fish and toss with two forks over high heat until very hot. Add cream, salt, pepper, and parsley, and taste for seasoning. Heat again until very hot and serve at once.

Baked Apples

12–14 Granny Smith or other tart apples
2.5 dl/½ pt/1 cup water
3.25 dl/¾ pt/1½ cups double cream, stiffly
  whipped (for serving)

For dried fruit filling
75 g/3 oz/½ cup raisins
75 g/3 oz/½ cup sultanas
75 g/3 oz/½ cup chopped mixed candied
  peel, chopped dried apricots, or chopped
  dates
175 g/6 oz/¾ cup butter
175 g/6 oz/¾ cup dark brown sugar

For chocolate filling
175–200 g/6–7 oz semi-sweet chocolate
1.8 dl/6 fl. oz/¾ cup golden syrup

You can bake as many or as few apples as
you like. Each of the above fillings is
enough for 12–14 apples, so if you want to
try both fillings, the quantities should be
halved.

Set the oven at moderately hot (190°C,
Mark 5, 375°F). Wipe the apples, remove
the cores with an apple corer or a rotary
vegetable peeler, and slit the skin horizontally around the middle of each apple to
prevent them from bursting. Set the apples
in 1–2 shallow baking dishes.

For dried fruit filling: Mix the dried fruits and
fill them into the cavities in the apples.
Cream the butter, beat in the sugar until
soft and fluffy, and top each apple with a
spoonful of the mixture. Pour 2.5 dl/½ pt/1
cup water around apples.

For chocolate filling: Break each square of
chocolate in half and fill each apple with
half a square. Spoon over the golden syrup
and add 2.5 dl/½ pt/1 cup water to the dish.
  Bake the apples in the heated oven for
30–35 minutes or until they are very tender
when pierced with a skewer. Serve warm
with whipped cream.

MENUS FOR TWENTY-FOUR

Kebab Barbecue

An Exotic Cocktail Party

A Traditional Buffet

An Outdoor Lunch

MENUS FOR TWENTY-FOUR

Parties for large numbers give you a chance to reunite old friends or to introduce different circles of friends to one another. You can also display your talent for matching menus to the setting – be it a splendid formal buffet indoors, a barbecue at which the guests help with the cooking, or a patio or poolside party.

An effortless way to entertain large numbers is at a Kebab Barbecue. If you provide tempting platters of the ingredients – shrimps, marinated lamb cubes, mushrooms, tomatoes, green peppers, and plenty of seasonings – you can leave the guests to assemble and grill their own kebabs, and do almost no cooking yourself. Some enthusiast can usually be found to take charge of the fire, and if you use paper plates and napkins, washing up can be kept to a minimum.

The standard Cocktail Party takes an exotic turn with informal hors d'oeuvre from the Middle East. These include Greek taramasalata (a spread made from fish roe) and baba ghanouj, an aubergine purée flavoured with garlic and lemon juice.

For a Traditional Buffet that dazzles the eye, it is hard to beat salmon in aspic with its sauces, salads, and garnishes, An informal alternative is the Outdoor Lunch of gazpacho soup and paella. This menu can, of course, be served indoors as well, but the aromatic spiciness of paella is particularly suited to the open air.

An alternative outdoor menu would be the Fork Lunch of antipasto, baked lasagne, and caramel pecan parfait suggested in Menus for Twelve; the recipes can easily be doubled for twenty-four people. Another Menu for Twelve easily doubled is the Brunch of kedgeree (the Indian rice dish with salmon and hard-boiled eggs) followed by baked apples. Canapés for a formal Cocktail Party are given in

Menus for Fifty so for twenty-four people, you can simply select your favourites.

Any kind of party for twenty-four people needs careful planning. Rather than use your own plates, cutlery, and dishes, you may prefer to hire them. A generous supply of ice for cocktails and tall drinks is a must. You will also need to plan guest space, and if the party takes place indoors, furniture will need rearranging. Outdoor parties are less confining, but remember to check that table tops and chair seats are clean and the patio or pool area is swept.

Kebab Barbecue

Shrimp Kebabs with Herbs
Marinated Lamb Kebabs
Saffron Rice Pilaf
Tarte au Citron
Tarte à l'Orange

A barbecue is one of the few meals for large numbers that you can manage without outside help. With good advance planning and a couple of hours of hard work preparing the ingredients and setting up the table, you can serve an excellent meal for twenty-four or more. Be sure to light the fire well ahead of cooking time so that it has time to reduce to the grey glow which is best for barbecuing.

The secret of delicious kebabs lies in a preliminary step – marinating overnight. A marinade not only helps prevent food from drying out during the cooking, but also adds taste. In this menu wine flavours the marinade for the lamb cubes, and a sherry and lemon mixture is perfect for the shrimps.

Skewers at the ready, your guests can compose and cook their kebabs to order. Provide whole mushrooms and pieces of onions with small tomatoes and squares of green and red pepper for colour. Many people like to thread bay leaf among the vegetables, so include a bowl of bay leaves broken into two or three pieces. With clearly labelled bowls of basting sauce, one for the lamb and the other for the shrimps, you can leave everyone to his own devices. Saffron rice pilaf is an ideal accompaniment.

The vibrant colours and flavours of fresh orange and lemon enliven these pastry desserts. Overlapping slices of the fruit conceal a rich almond filling. To save yourself trouble when slicing the oranges, look for the seedless navel variety – they have a 'navel' break in the skin at one end. Seedless lemons are harder to detect – it is mainly a matter of luck, but good juicy lemons have smooth, bright yellow skins and feel resilient, rather than hard, to the touch. Both orange and lemon tarts (each is made twice, so there are four flans in all) can be prepared 5–6 hours ahead.

COUNTDOWN

Day Before
Cut up lamb, add marinade, and keep
    tightly covered.
Add marinade to shrimps and keep
    covered.
Make saffron rice pilaf and leave in pan
    for reheating.
Make pastry for tartes, bake shells, and
    keep in an airtight container.

5–6 Hours Before Serving
Prepare vegetables for kebabs, pile in
    bowls, and keep covered.
Fill pastry shells and complete orange
    and lemon tarts.
Make herb butter for shrimps.

1 Hour Before Serving
Light barbecue fire.
Set oven at moderate (180°C, Mark 4,
    350°F).

45 Minutes Before Serving
Put rice in oven to reheat.

15 Minutes Before Serving
Drain lamb cubes and reserve marinade
    for basting.
Heat herb butter for shrimps.
Carry all kebab ingredients to table and
    arrange them; set lamb marinade and
    herb butter beside barbecue grill.
Put rice on table burner or corner of grill
    to keep hot.

After Serving Kebabs
Bring out orange and lemon tarts.

Shrimp Kebabs with Herbs

$2\frac{1}{4}$ kg / 5 lb uncooked large shrimps, peeled
assorted vegetables (see page 153)

For marinade
5 dl / 1 pt / / 2 cups oil
1.25 dl / $\frac{1}{4}$ pt / $\frac{1}{2}$ cup sherry
1 tbs lemon juice
1 tsp freshly ground black pepper

For herb butter
2.25 g / $\frac{1}{2}$ lb / 1 cup butter
2 tbs chopped parsley
1 tbs chopped chives
1 tsp thyme
1 tsp oregano or basil
salt and freshly ground black pepper

This recipe can be doubled or halved; served
alone, it is enough for twelve people.

For the marinade: Whisk the oil a teaspoon
at a time into the sherry, lemon juice, and
black pepper so that the marinade emulsifies
and thickens slightly. Pour over the shrimps
in a bowl (not aluminium) and mix well.
Cover tightly and chill overnight.

For the herb butter: Melt the butter, then
chill until solidified and discard the milky
liquid at the bottom (this clarifies the
butter). Melt the clarified butter, add the
parsley, chives, thyme, oregano or basil,
and a little salt and pepper, and keep warm.
    Drain the shrimps, thread them on kebab
skewers with other ingredients of your
choice (see page 153), brush with herb
butter, and grill 5–8 cm / 2–3 inches from
the coals for 2–3 minutes on each side or
until the shrimps are slightly browned;
brush often with herb butter during
cooking.

Marinated Lamb Kebabs

$2\frac{1}{4}$–$2\frac{3}{4}$ kg/5–6 lb boneless lean leg of lamb
assorted vegetables (see below)

For marinade
3.25 dl/$\frac{3}{4}$ pt/1$\frac{1}{2}$ cups red wine
1.25 dl/$\frac{1}{4}$ pt/$\frac{1}{2}$ cup oil
2 onions, sliced
2 carrots, sliced
2 cloves garlic, crushed
10–12 peppercorns
bouquet garni

This recipe, served alone, is enough for
twelve; you can double or halve it.

Cut the lamb into 2$\frac{1}{2}$-cm/1-inch cubes, discarding all fat and gristle.

For the marinade: In a large saucepan (not
aluminium) bring the red wine, oil, onions,
carrots, garlic, peppercorns, and bouquet
garni to the boil; cover and let stand till
cool. Strain the marinade over the lamb,
mix well, cover tightly, and keep in the
refrigerator for at least 12 hours and up to
36 hours, stirring the mixture from time to
time.

Drain the lamb cubes, reserving the
marinade, and thread them on skewers
with any of the ingredients suggested
below. Grill the kebabs 8–10 cm/3–4 inches
from the coals, allowing 4–5 minutes on
each side and brushing the kebabs with
marinade during cooking.

Suggested Additions for Kebabs

For twenty-four people
1$\frac{1}{2}$ kg/3 lb tomatoes
1$\frac{1}{2}$ kg/3 lb small mushrooms, stems trimmed
5–6 large onions, roots trimmed, quartered,
  and pulled apart into leaves
5–6 green peppers, cored, seeded, and cut in
  4-cm/1$\frac{1}{2}$-inch squares
5–6 red peppers, cored, seeded, and cut in
  4-cm/1$\frac{1}{2}$-inch squares
2 packages bay leaves, torn in 2–3 pieces

Pile the ingredients in separate bowls for
guests to help themselves.

Saffron Rice Pilaf

225 g/½ lb/1 cup butter
6 onions, chopped
1½ kg/3¼ lb/7 cups rice
½ tsp saffron, soaked in 2.5 dl/½ pt/1 cup hot
    water
3 l/6 pt/13 cups water
salt and pepper

Even in this large quantity, pilaf reheats
well; a smaller recipe is given in the Quick
Supper in Menus for Six.

In a very large casserole (or two smaller
ones) melt the butter and sauté the onion
until soft but not brown. Add the rice and
cook, stirring, for 1–2 minutes until the
grains are transparent. Add the saffron and
liquid, water, salt and pepper, cover and
bring to the boil. Simmer on top of the
stove or cook in a moderate oven (180°C,
Mark 4, 350°F) for 25–30 minutes or until
all the water is absorbed. Let the rice cool
15 minutes before stirring it with a fork to
fluff up the grains.

 To reheat: Put the rice, covered, in a
moderate oven (180°C, Mark 4, 350°F) for
40–50 minutes (for the large casserole) or
25–35 minutes (for two smaller ones), or
heat it gently on top of the stove until very
hot. At the barbecue, keep the rice hot on a
table burner or at the side of the barbecue
grill.

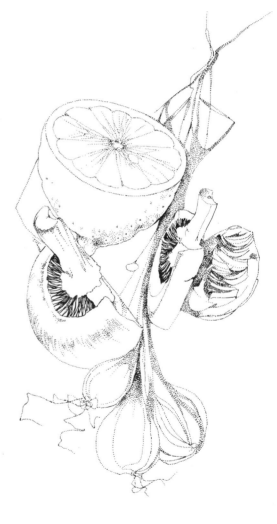

Tarte au Citron

French pie pastry made with 400 g/14 oz/3
   cups flour, pinch of salt, 200 g/7 oz/⅔ cup
   butter, 150 g/5 oz/¾ cup sugar, 6 egg
   yolks, 1½ tsp vanilla (see page 114)
icing sugar (for sprinkling)
1 thinly sliced lemon (for decoration,
   optional)

For the filling
6 eggs
300 g/11 oz/1½ cups sugar
grated rind and juice of 4 lemons
300 g/11 oz/1½ cups melted butter
200 g/7 oz/1¼ cups whole blanched
   almonds, ground

*Two 25–30 cm/10–12 inch tart tins or flan
rings*

This recipe makes 2 tarts, so you can easily
halve the quantity.

Make the French pie pastry: Line into the
tins or rings and bake empty as for regular
pastry (page 51), cooking only 15 minutes,
not the full 25 minutes. Transfer to a rack
to cool.

For the filling: Beat the eggs and sugar until
light and thick enough to leave a ribbon
trail when the whisk is lifted. Stir in the
lemon juice and rind, followed by the
melted butter and ground almonds. Pour
the mixture into the pie shells and bake in
the heated oven (180°C, Mark 4, 350°F)
25–30 minutes, or until the filling is golden
brown and set. Let the pies cool.
   Just before serving, sprinkle the pies with
icing sugar and, if you like, decorate them
with very thin slices of lemon.

Tarte à L'Orange

Follow the recipe for lemon tarte, substituting the grated rind and juice of 3
oranges for the lemons and adding 1 tablespoon Grand Marnier to the filling. After the
pies are baked, sprinkle each with 1 tablespoon Grand Marnier.

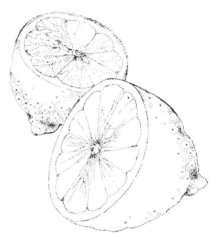

An Exotic Cocktail Party

Taramasalata
Hummos bi Tahina
Baba Ghanouj
Dolmas with Yogurt
Pita Bread
Vegetable Sticks
Greek or Italian-style Olives

In the Middle East, hors d'oeuvre are an institution. No one pauses for a quick glass of *arak*, the potent local spirit, without nibbling a few olives or pistachios. The standard opening to any meal is an array of little dishes – the more the better – which may include stuffed baby aubergines, pickled peppers, and slices of feta cheese. Many of these Middle Eastern specialities are ideal for a Western-style cocktail party.

In much the same way as we serve dips and crackers, Middle Easterners eat several fish and vegetable purées with torn fragments of pita bread. The Greek speciality is taramasalata, made with smoked fish roe that is beaten with lemon juice, olive oil, and breadcrumbs into a deliciously light fluffy spread. Another purée, hummos bi tahina, is made of chick-peas and sesame paste. Also found all over the Middle East is baba ghanouj, baked aubergine – often called poor man's caviar because of its pearly grey colour – which is mashed with garlic, sesame oil, and lemon juice. Incidentally, these purées, particularly the hummos, are also good served with sticks of raw vegetables instead of bread for dipping.

Dolmas usually refers to vine leaves, filled with rice and meat and flavoured with lemon. The word comes from the Turkish for 'to stuff' and even gives its name to the communal taxis, invariably filled to overflowing, called dolmus.

Flat chewy pita bread, also known as Syrian bread, is the universal accompaniment to Middle Eastern hors d'oeuvre. With them also comes goat's milk yogurt for dipping, or spooning over food as a sauce. It adds flavour but also has a practical advantage of keeping food moist – like the common habit of spooning a little olive oil over yogurt and on all purées. All these Middle Eastern dishes can be prepared in advance, and they stand up well to summer temperatures. They have to; after all, they were created for the hot climate of the Eastern Mediterranean.

You should not have much trouble finding the ingredients for these dishes. Most big cities have Middle Eastern stores; good grocers have some things like vine leaves in brine, while health food stores have chick-peas and goat's milk yogurt.

Two of these recipes – the taramasalata and hummos – demand a blender to grind the ingredients to a smooth, light purée, unless you care to spend hours working by hand. Alternatively, make double quantities of dolmas and baba ghanouj, which require little beating.

COUNTDOWN

Several Days Before
Make taramasalata and hummos bi
  tahina and keep tightly covered.

Day Before Serving
Make baba ghanouj and dolmas and
  keep tightly covered.

In the Morning
Cut vegetable sticks for baba ghanouj
  and keep in ice water.

1 Hour Before Serving
Pile taramasalata, hummos bi tahina,
  and baba ghanouj in bowls, and add
  garnish.
Arrange dolmas on a platter.
Put yogurt in a bowl for dipping.
Arrange vegetables on a platter.
Put assorted Greek or Italian-style olives
  in bowls.
Set oven at moderate (180°C, Mark 4,
  350°F).

Just Before or During Party
Heat pita bread for 2 minutes in oven
  until lightly browned and tear into
  pieces for serving.

Taramasalata

3 slices bread, crusts removed
2.5 dl/$\frac{1}{4}$pt/$\frac{1}{2}$ cup water or milk
250 g/$\frac{1}{2}$lb tarama (smoked cod's roe)
3 tbs lemon juice
2.5 dl/$\frac{1}{2}$pt/1 cup olive oil
freshly ground black pepper

For garnish
1–2 tsp olive oil
1 tbs chopped parsley (optional)

This recipe can be doubled, but the ingredients must be puréed only a little at a
time in the blender. Taramasalata keeps for
4–5 days in the refrigerator.

Soak the bread in water for 5 minutes and
gently squeeze out any excess liquid. *If the
tarama tastes very salty, use milk instead of
water to counteract the salt.* Work half the
tarama a little at a time in a blender at
medium speed, with some of the bread and
lemon juice; add half the oil a teaspoon at a
time. Add pepper and transfer to a bowl.
Blend the remaining ingredients in the same
way and taste, adding more pepper and
lemon juice if necessary.

  For serving, pile in a bowl, spoon over
olive oil, and sprinkle with parsley if you
like. Serve with pita bread (page 29) or
crackers.

Hummos bi Tahina

225 g/$\frac{1}{2}$ lb/1 cup dried chick-peas, soaked
   overnight and drained
1.25 dl/$\frac{1}{4}$ pt/$\frac{1}{2}$ cup lemon juice or to taste
2–3 cloves garlic, crushed
175 g/6 oz/$\frac{3}{4}$ cup tahina (sesame) paste
salt and freshly ground black pepper

For garnish
2–3 tsp olive oil
1 teaspoon paprika

You can easily double this recipe, but don't
try to work too much in the blender at
once. The purée keeps well for up to a week
in the refrigerator.

Put the chick-peas in a pan with water, to
cover, add a lid, and simmer 1$\frac{1}{4}$–1$\frac{1}{2}$ hours
until they are very tender. Drain, reserving
the cooking liquid. Purée some chick-peas a
little at a time in a blender with some of the
lemon juice, garlic, tahina paste, salt and
pepper, adding enough cooking liquid to
make a mixture that will just fall from a
spoon. Transfer to a bowl and purée remaining ingredients in the same way.
Combine them and taste for seasoning, adding more salt, pepper, lemon juice, or garlic
to taste.

   For serving, pile the hummos bi tahina in
a bowl, spoon over a little olive oil and
sprinkle with paprika. Serve with pita bread
or sticks of fresh carrot, celery, and courgettes (page 159).

Baba Ghanouj

1 medium aubergine
1 small onion, very finely chopped
2 cloves garlic, crushed
4 tbs olive or sesame oil
2–3 tbs lemon juice
salt and freshly ground black pepper
1 tbs chopped parsley (for garnish)

This recipe can easily be doubled. It keeps
well in the refrigerator for a day or two.

Grill the whole aubergine, turning it often,
for about 20 minutes or until the skin is
charred and the flesh is tender. *If possible
use a charcoal grill to add a smoky flavour.*
Peel the aubergine under cold water and
squeeze out as much of the juice as possible.
In a bowl mash the flesh thoroughly with a
potato masher, then beat in the onion and
garlic. Beat in the oil, a little at a time, and
2 tablespoons of the lemon juice. Add salt
and pepper to taste and more lemon juice if
needed.

   For serving, pile the baba ghanouj in a
bowl and sprinkle with chopped parsley.
Serve with pita bread.

Pita Bread

You can buy pita bread in Middle Eastern
stores and some supermarkets. Allow
10–12/18-cm/7-inch rounds for serving
with cocktails for twenty-four. Just before
serving, bake the bread in a moderate oven
(180°C, Mark 4, 350°F) for 2 minutes until
hot, or heat according to package directions. Tear the bread into large pieces, pile
in a bowl, and serve at once.

Dolmas with Yogurt

---

250 g/9 oz vine leaves in brine
1.25 dl/$\frac{1}{4}$ pt/$\frac{1}{2}$ cup olive oil
2 onions, chopped
450 g/1 lb minced beef or lamb
250 g/$\frac{1}{2}$ lb/1 cup rice
2 cloves garlic, crushed
1 tsp ground cumin
1 tsp ground allspice
2 tbs pine nuts (optional)
salt and freshly ground black pepper
4 tbs/$\frac{1}{4}$ cup lemon juice
$\frac{3}{4}$–1 l/1$\frac{1}{2}$–2 pt/3–4 cups water
5 dl/1 pt/2 cups goat's milk yogurt or plain
    cow's milk yogurt (for serving)

This recipe can easily be doubled, and dolmas keep well in the refrigerator for 3–4 days. They can also be served hot as an entrée. Makes about 60 dolmas.

Drain the vine leaves, put them in a large bowl, and cover with plenty of boiling water, separating the leaves as much as possible. Let soak $\frac{1}{2}$ hour, drain, rinse with cold water, and drain again on paper towels.

For the filling: In a frying pan heat 2 table-spoons oil and fry the onion until soft but not brown. Add the meat and cook, stirring, until browned. Take from the heat and stir in the rice, garlic, cumin, allspice, pine nuts, if used, and plenty of salt and pepper.

   Put a teaspoon of filling on the dull side of each vine leaf and roll up from the base, folding in the edges to make a neat parcel; roll back and forth under your hand to form a cylinder. Use all the filling, but reserve a few leaves. Lay these leaves in a shallow saucepan to prevent sticking and pack the dolmas tightly on top. Sprinkle with lemon juice and the remaining oil and pour over $\frac{3}{4}$ l/1$\frac{1}{2}$ pt/3 cups water.

   Set a heatproof plate on top to weigh down the dolmas, cover, and simmer on top of the stove for 1$\frac{1}{4}$ hours or until the dolmas are firm. Add more water during cooking if the dolmas look dry. Let cool and keep in the cooking liquid. An hour or two before serving, drain the dolmas, spear them with toothpicks, arrange on a platter, and serve with the yogurt.

Vegetable Sticks

For twenty-four people, cut 450 g/1 pound peeled carrots, 1 bunch celery, and 450 g/1 pound courgettes (unpeeled) in 5-cm/2-inch sticks. Soak carrot and celery in ice water for at least 1 hour; keep courgettes in plastic wrap. Drain before serving.

A Traditional Buffet

Salmon in Aspic

Green Mayonnaise

Mayonnaise Chantilly

Potato Vinaigrette

Fresh Asparagus Salad

Stuffed Eggs

Lemon Mousse with
Caramel Sauce

Strawberry Almond Torte

Half the glory of a traditional buffet is its appearance – shining silver, smooth white linen, and serried rows of glasses provide a fine background for the display of food.

A sumptuous platter of salmon in aspic, embellished with scales of cucumber and flanked by tomato boats amply repays your time. Preparation must begin at least a day in advance, and cutting the decorations and adding the coats of aspic call for care and patience – you will find advice on using aspic in the introduction to a Formal Buffet in Menus for Fifty as well as exact instructions in the following recipe.

One shortcut suggested here is to make a quick aspic with tinned consommé; so little of the aspic is served with each portion of the fish that only your most discerning guests will notice it isn't homemade. If you do want to spend time making your own aspic, any classic French cookbook describes it in detail. Once complete, the salmon in aspic can be kept for up to a day in the refrigerator without harm.

Salmon for twenty-four people is an expensive treat, and it is well worth taking the trouble to get the best. Fresh salmon is at its peak in spring and early summer, though some markets have fresh salmon for most of the year. Many fishmongers have stocks of frozen salmon, but its flavour does not equal that of the fresh fish. Be sure to order the fish well beforehand and ask the fishmonger to leave the head on so that the salmon can be decorated attractively. For serving twenty-four people, you should allow about 350 g/¾ lb per person. Leftover salmon pieces make delectable salads or mousses for smaller meals.

Stuffed eggs, flavoured with tomato or a

COUNTDOWN

3–4 Days Before
Make and bake almond pastry rounds;
  store in airtight container.

2 Days Before
Make mayonnaise, but do not add herbs
  or cream; keep covered.
Make vinaigrette dressing for potatoes
  and for asparagus.
Poach salmon and chill, make aspic.

Day Before
Prepare cucumber and tomato baskets
  for salmon and chill.
Complete salmon in aspic and cover
  loosely with plastic wrap.
Hard-boil 31 eggs. Finely chop 3 eggs for
  asparagus vinaigrette and keep
  covered. With remaining eggs make
  fillings for stuffed eggs and cover. Keep
  whites in cold water at room temperature.

Chop shallot or spring onion and parsley
  for asparagus and keep covered.
Boil potatoes, peel and complete potato
  vinaigrette; keep covered.
Make lemon mousse and cover tightly.

3–4 Hours Before Serving
Complete green mayonnaise, cover and
  keep at room temperature.
Fill hard-boiled eggs, arrange on platter,
  and keep covered at room temperature.
Cook asparagus and keep covered on
  platters. Finish dressing, but do not
  coat asparagus.
Let potato vinaigrette come to room
  temperature.
Assemble and decorate almond torte.

1 Hour Before Serving
Garnish salmon platters with watercress.
Complete mayonnaise Chantilly and
  cover.
Spoon dressing over asparagus salad.
Unmould lemon mousse and decorate.

devil mixture, will complement the salmon as well as make it go further, while potato vinaigrette is an excellent accompaniment, less rich than the usual potato salad made with mayonnaise. The flavour improves if the salad is made ahead so that the potatoes have time to marinate in the dressing.

Fresh asparagus is an early summer treat that happily coincides with the salmon season. It is incomparable when you can get it, so don't be tempted by the second best of tinned or frozen asparagus. Instead, serve a green salad made with your favourite lettuce.

The two desserts in this menu are flavoured with fruit to provide a contrast to the richness of the salmon. The cold mousse is light and pleasantly tart with lemon and the crisp almond torte can be layered with fresh strawberries or fresh peaches, depending on the season.

Salmon in Aspic

2 whole salmon (about $4\frac{1}{2}$ kg / 10 lb each), cleaned, with heads and tails left on

For poaching
5 dl / 1 pt / 2 cups white wine
1.25 dl / $\frac{1}{4}$ pt / $\frac{1}{2}$ cup white wine vinegar
2 onions, sliced
12 peppercorns
2–3 large sprigs parsley
3–4 l / 6–8 pt water

For garnish
7–8 cucumbers
salt and pepper
24 even-sized tomatoes
2 kg / 4 lb large shrimps, cooked
4 bunches watercress

For aspic
35 g / $1\frac{1}{2}$ oz / 3 envelopes gelatine
six 300 g / $10\frac{1}{2}$ oz tins beef consommé
4 tbs brandy
4 tbs sherry

fish kettle

You can halve or double the quantities of this recipe, but you will need the same amount of court bouillon. If you haven't a fish kettle, use a rack in a large roasting pan and cover with foil instead of a lid.

One to two days before the party, poach the salmon: Set 1 fish, stomach down, on the rack of a fish kettle and tie it in place with string. Put the rack in the pan, add the white wine, wine vinegar, onions, peppercorns, parsley, and water to almost cover the fish. Cover with the lid and bring slowly to the boil; this should take about 20 minutes. Simmer for 30 minutes (50 minutes total cooking time, or 5 minutes per pound of fish), then let the fish cool to tepid in the liquid.

Lift it out, peel off the skin and remove the fins, leaving on head and tail. Scoop out the small bones along the spine and transfer the fish to a large platter or silver tray. Cool the cooking liquid completely and cook the other fish in the liquid in the same way. Cover both fish and chill thoroughly, preferably overnight.

The next day, prepare the garnish and aspic: Peel 2 of the cucumbers lengthwise leaving strips of green peel so they look striped; slice the cucumbers very thinly. Arrange slices overlapping on the salmon to resemble scales and chill.

Peel, seed, and dice the remaining cucumbers, sprinkle them with salt and let stand 30 minutes to draw out the juices. Rinse them with cold water and drain on paper towels.

To make tomato baskets: Core the tomatoes, set them on a board, core side down, and make 2 parallel vertical cuts to halfway down the tomatoes and remove 2 wedges from the sides, leaving a handle in the middle. Scoop out the seeds and sprinkle the insides of the tomatoes with salt and pepper. Fill the tomatoes with the diced cucumbers and chill thoroughly.

To make the aspic: Sprinkle the gelatine over 1 tin consommé in a pan and let stand 5 minutes until spongy. Melt it over gentle heat and stir into the remaining consommé with the brandy and sherry. Pour a thin layer of aspic around each salmon on the platters and chill until set.

Pour about 5 dl/1 pt of the remaining aspic into a metal bowl and set it over another bowl filled with ice. Stir it very gently with a large metal spoon until the consistency is oily (vigorous stirring makes the aspic bubbly) and it is about to set. *It sets quickly, so you must work fast.* Spoon a coating of aspic over both salmon and chill.

Arrange the tomato baskets along one side of each salmon platter, overlap the shrimps along the other side, and chill. Melt any solidified aspic in the metal bowl, add more aspic, and chill again over ice, Repeat the coating process, covering the 2 salmon and the garnish and chill them. Give them a final coating of aspic and chill well. When firmly set, cover with plastic wrap. *Do not let the salmon get too cold or the aspic will crystallize. You can prepare 24 hours ahead up to this point.*

Just before serving, garnish each platter with watercress.

Mayonnaise Chantilly

5 dl/1 pt/2 cups mayonnaise (page 45)
2.5 dl/$\frac{1}{2}$ pt/1 cup double cream, whipped
    until it holds a soft shape
juice $\frac{1}{2}$ lemon
salt and pepper

Not more than 2 hours before serving, fold the whipped cream into the mayonnaise with the lemon juice and taste for seasoning.

Green Mayonnaise

1 l/1$\frac{3}{4}$ pt/4 cups mayonnaise (page 45)
1 bunch watercress, stems removed
4 or 5 cups parsley sprigs
2 tbs chopped chives or several stems of dill
salt and pepper

Put 5 dl/1 pt/2 cups mayonnaise in a blender with the watercress, parsley sprigs, and chives or dill, and work until finely chopped. Stir into the remaining mayonnaise and taste for seasoning. Alternatively, finely chop the herbs and watercress and stir them into the mayonnaise. Let stand at least 2 hours before using.

Potato Vinaigrette

$3\frac{1}{2}$–$4\frac{1}{2}$ kg/8–10 lb small new potatoes
1 1/2 pt/4 cups vinaigrette dressing
   (page 41)
2 tbs chopped chives (optional)

This salad can be made up to 24 hours
ahead. You can halve or double the recipe.

Cook the potatoes in their skins in boiling
water for 15–20 minutes or until they are
just tender when pierced with a knife. Drain
them and peel while still warm. If using
chives, add them to the vinaigrette dressing.
Pour over the dressing and mix carefully so
the potatoes are coated. *Adding the dressing
to the potatoes while still warm gives them
more flavour.* Taste the salad, add more
seasoning if necessary, cover, and let cool.
Pile in serving dishes and serve at room
temperature.

Fresh Asparagus Salad

225 g/8 lb fresh asparagus
5 dl/1 pt/2 cups vinaigrette dressing
   (page 41)
3 hard-boiled eggs, finely chopped
5 shallots or white part of 5 spring onions,
   finely chopped
2 tbs chopped parsley

This recipe is easy to halve; if you double it,
cook the asparagus in at least two batches.

Cut off the hard ends of the asparagus and
peel the lower part of the stems with a
vegetable peeler. Tie the stems in bundles
and set them upright in a large kettle, Add
about $2\frac{1}{2}$ cm/1 inch of salted water to the
pan, cover, and bring to the boil. In this
way the tough stems cook quickly in water
and the delicate tops are steamed. Cook for
8–10 minutes until the tops are just tender.
Drain and run under cold water to set the
colour; drain again thoroughly.

For the dressing: Stir the hard-boiled eggs,
shallots or spring onions, and parsley into
the vinaigrette dressing. Taste for seasoning.
*You can prepare 4 hours ahead up to this
point.*
   Arrange the asparagus in neat piles on
dishes and remove the strings. Spoon the
dressing over the centre of the asparagus,
leaving the tips and ends of asparagus un-
coated.

Stuffed Eggs

28 hard-boiled eggs
1–2 bunches watercress (for garnish)

For tomato filling
225 g/$\frac{1}{2}$/1 cup butter, softened
1.25 dl/$\frac{1}{4}$pt/$\frac{1}{2}$ cup tomato paste
salt and pepper

For devilled filling
2.5 dl/$\frac{1}{2}$pt/1 cup mayonnaise (page 45)
1 tbs anchovy paste
1 tsp Worcestershire sauce (or to taste)
few drops Tabasco sauce or pinch of
   cayenne (or to taste)

icing bag and medium star nozzle

This recipe can be halved or doubled.

Peel the eggs; cut them in half lengthwise
and scoop out the yolks.

For tomato filling: Work half the yolks
through a sieve into the butter and beat
until smooth with the tomato paste and salt
and pepper to taste.

For devilled filling: Work the remaining yolks
through a sieve into the mayonnaise and
beat in anchovy paste, Worcestershire
sauce, Tabasco or cayenne, adding more to
taste. Cover the yolk mixtures and store
separately in the refrigerator. Keep the egg
whites in a bowl of cold water at room temperature. *You can prepare 24 hours ahead up
to this point.*

You can fill the eggs up to 4 hours before
serving. Let the yolk mixtures come to room
temperature if they are stiff; drain and pat
the egg whites dry on paper towels. Fill
each mixture into an icing bag fitted with a
star nozzle and pipe into the egg whites,
mounding the mixture well. Arrange the
eggs on dishes and keep loosely covered at
room temperature. Garnish with watercress
just before serving.

Lemon Mousse with Caramel Sauce

For the mousse
8 eggs
6 egg yolks
225 g/½ lb/1 cup sugar
grated rind and juice of 6 lemons
25 g/1 oz/2 envelopes gelatine
2.5 dl/½ pt/1 cup water
7.5 dl/1½ pt/3 cups double cream, whipped
    until it holds a soft shape
5 dl/1 pt/2 cups double cream, stiffly
    whipped (for decoration)

For caramel sauce
700 g/1½ lb/3 cups sugar
5 dl/2 pt/2 cups cold water
5 dl/2 pt/2 cups warm water

*2 ring moulds (1½ l/3 pt capacity each); icing
bag and medium star nozzle*

This recipe serves twelve people, and with
the strawberry almond torte, it is enough
for twenty-four. The mousse must be made
in 2 batches, as the eggs are hard to beat,
but the caramel sauce for twelve can be
made at one time.

Lightly oil the ring mould.
    In a bowl combine 4 eggs and 3 egg
yolks and gradually beat in 100 g/¼ lb/½ cup
sugar. Heat the grated lemon rind and juice
of 3 lemons until hot but not boiling and
stir into the egg yolk mixture. If you are
using a rotary beater, set the bowl over a

pan of simmering water and beat about 10
minutes or until the mixture is light and
thick enough to leave a ribbon trail when
the beater is lifted. Take from the heat and
continue beating until the mixture is cool. If
you are using an electric beater, no heat is
necessary.
    Sprinkle 4 level teaspoons gelatine over
1.25 dl/¼ pt/½ cup water in a small pan and
let stand 5 minutes until spongy. Melt over
gentle heat and stir into the lemon mixture.
Set the bowl over a pan of ice water and
chill, stirring occasionally, until the mixture
starts to set. When the mixture is on the
point of setting, fold in half of the lightly
whipped cream and pour the mousse into
the mould. Cover and chill at least 2 hours
or until firmly set. Make a second mousse
in the same way with the remaining
ingredients.

To make the caramel sauce: Heat the sugar
gently with the cold water until dissolved,
bring to the boil, and cook steadily to a rich
brown caramel. *The caramel must be well
browned or it will be unpleasantly sweet, but
do not let it burn or it will turn bitter.* Take
from the heat and at once add the warm
water, standing back because the caramel
will sputter. Heat gently until the caramel is
melted and let cool. *You can prepare 24
hours ahead up to this point.*
    Up to 2 hours before serving: Run a small
knife around the edge of the mousse to release the airlock and unmould it onto a
dish. Put the stiffly whipped cream in an
icing bag fitted with a star nozzle and
decorate the mousse with rosettes. Keep in
the refrigerator. Serve the caramel sauce
separately.

Strawberry Almond Torte

350 g/¾ lb/2¾ cups whole blanched almonds
225 g/½ lb/1 cup butter
225 g/½ lb/1 cup sugar
175 g/6 oz/1½ cups flour

For the filling
4 tbs brandy or 2 tsp vanilla
4 tbs sugar or to taste
7.5 dl/1½ pt/3 cups double cream, whipped
    until it holds a soft shape
3 kg/7 lb fresh strawberries, hulled

icing bag and medium star nozzle

This recipe serves twelve people; it can
easily be halved, but double the quantity of
almond pastry is hard to handle.

Bake the almonds in a moderately hot oven
(190°C, Mark 5, 375°F) for 10–12 minutes
or until lightly browned. Grind them in a
rotary cheese grater or work them in a
blender, a few at a time, until finely ground.

Cream the butter, beat in the sugar, and
continue beating until soft and light. Stir in
the ground almonds and flour and work to
a smooth dough. Chill ½–1 hour. Set the
oven at moderately hot (190°C, Mark 5,
375°F).

Divide the dough into six portions, and
with the heel of the hand, pat each portion
out on a baking sheet to a 18–21-cm/7–8-
inch round. Bake in the heated oven for
10–12 minutes or until golden brown.
While they are still warm, trim the rounds
neatly with a knife, using a plate or pan lid
as a guide; cut two rounds into 8 wedges.
Transfer to racks to cool; store in airtight
containers. *You can prepare 4–5 days ahead
up to this point.*

Not more than 4 hours before serving,
beat the brandy or vanilla and sugar into
the whipped cream and continue beating
until stiff. Reserve about 3.25 dl/¾ pt/
1½ cups cream and 16 strawberries for decoration. Halve the remaining strawberries
through the stem. Set a pastry round on a
dish, spread it with a quarter of the cream,
and top with a quarter of the halved strawberries. Set another pastry round on top and
add a third of the remaining strawberries
and cream. Top with a round of pastry
wedges. Assemble the other torte in the
same way.

Put the reserved cream into an icing bag
fitted with a star nozzle, and top each
pastry wedge at the edge with a rosette of
cream. Put a strawberry on each rosette
and chill torte until serving.

An Outdoor Lunch

Gazpacho
Paella
Green Salad
Flan

Food for dining outdoors must be simple, with clear colours and forceful flavours to compete with the attraction of the surroundings. From Spain comes an ideal sequence of dishes – the piquant soup called gazpacho, the peasant dish of paella, and the popular caramel custard dessert, flan. Both soup and flan are made ahead and chilled, and the paella can be assembled before guests arrive, to be cooked at the last minute.

Gazpacho comes from Andalusia and La Mancha, and in these provinces you will find literally dozens of versions, most of them based on tomatoes, cucumbers, and green peppers, generously seasoned with

garlic. Almost like a liquid salad, gazpacho is diluted with iced water and ice cubes and served with a garnish of cubed vegetables and crunchy bread croûtons.

Follow this with the hearty paella – a peasant creation that began as a midday meal cooked over a makeshift open fire in the fields. Good paella is spicy without being hot, and the key to making this dish is to balance the ingredients so that no single flavour predominates. Layer your ingredients in the pan so that those requiring the most cooking lie on the bottom, nearest the heat, and top off with quick-cooking mussels or clams. The chicken must be partially sautéed in oil beforehand because it does not cook as fast as the other ingredients.

Cook paella fast at a steady boil so that the rice will absorb the liquid quickly and the grains remain separate and fluffy. The traditional shallow paella pan is ideal for this, but whatever the cooking vessel, take care not to let the heat scorch the bottom of the pan. Paella can be cooked very well in traditional style outdoors on a barbecue.

Flan means different things in different parts of the world. English-speaking countries think of an open pie filled with fruit, but for Spain and Latin America, flan is a rich caramel custard. It is one of the few Spanish desserts – most of their meals end with fresh fruit – and it is so popular it has become virtually the national dessert. In the south it is sometimes made with fresh orange juice instead of milk. But traditional flans are made with a custard of eggs, milk, and sugar that is baked in a caramel-lined dish. When turned out, the caramel colours the top of the flan and forms a light sauce.

COUNTDOWN

Day Before
Make gazpacho, but do not add ice
    water; keep covered.
Make garnish and keep covered in sepa-
    rate bowls.
Wash greens for salad and keep in plastic
    bag; make vinaigrette dressing.
Make caramel custard and keep, covered,
    in the moulds.

3–4 Hours Before Serving
Prepare all ingredients for paella.

1–2 Hours Before Serving
Assemble paella, but do not cook it. Light
    fire if cooking paella over a barbecue.
Unmould caramel custards and keep
    covered with plastic wrap.
Toast bread and cut in cubes for gazpacho
    croûtons; pile in a serving bowl.

30 Minutes Before Serving
Cook paella.

Just Before Serving
Toss green salad.
Add ice water and ice to gazpacho, and
    taste for seasoning.

Gazpacho

6 green peppers, cored, seeded, and chopped
4 cucumbers, peeled, seeded, and chopped
18 tomatoes, peeled, seeded, and chopped
    (page 207)
1 large onion, chopped
2 cloves garlic, crushed (optional)
1.75 dl/6 fl. oz olive oil
4 tbs wine vinegar
salt and pepper
8 slices white bread (for croûtons)
3 1/6 pt ice water
ice cubes (for serving)

Without a blender this soup is tedious to
make and the consistency is not so smooth.
The recipe can easily be halved or doubled.

Reserve 175 g/6 oz/2 cups each of the green
peppers, cucumbers, and tomatoes for
garnish. Purée the remaining peppers,
cucumbers, and tomatoes a little at a time
in a blender with the onion and garlic, if
used. Mix the purée thoroughly together in
a bowl. Alternatively, work the ingredients
through a food mill. Stir in the olive oil and
vinegar with plenty of salt and pepper.
Cover and chill. *You can prepare 24 hours
ahead up to this point.*

For the croûtons: Toast the bread and cut it
in cubes, discarding the crusts.
    A short time before serving, stir the ice
water and ice cubes into the soup and taste
for seasoning. As garnish serve the reserved
chopped peppers, cucumbers, and tomatoes
with the croûtons in separate dishes.

Paella

---

5 dozen mussels
5 dl/1 pt/2 cups olive oil
26–28 (about 3 kg/6 lb) chicken thighs or
    legs
6 onions, chopped
2 green peppers, cored, seeded, and cut in
    strips
2 kg/4 lb/8 cups rice
3 l/6 pts/12 cups chicken stock or water
1 tsp saffron, soaked in $\frac{1}{2}$ cup hot water for
    20 minutes
salt and freshly ground black pepper
1 kg/2 lb cleaned squid, sliced (optional)
1 kg/2 lb uncooked smoked ham, cut in
    strips
1 kg/2 lb chorizo sausages, thinly sliced
8 tomatoes, peeled, seeded, and cut in strips
    (see page 207)
1 kg/2 lb white fish fillets (cod, haddock, or
    bass), cut in strips
1–1$\frac{1}{2}$ kg/2–3 lb uncooked unpeeled shrimps

*2 large paella pans (46–51 cm/18–20 inches in
diameter) or shallow flameproof casseroles*

This recipe can be halved to cook in one
pan or doubled to cook in four pans.

Scrub the mussels or clams under running
water, and remove any weed. Discard any
with broken shells or with open shells that
do not close when tapped.

In each pan: Heat 2.5 dl/$\frac{1}{2}$ pt/1 cup oil
and brown half the chicken pieces on all
sides over medium heat for 10–12 minutes
so they are partly cooked. Take them out,
add half the onion and green pepper and
cook until soft. Add 1 kg/2 lb/4 cups rice to
each pan and cook, stirring, until the grains
are transparent and the oil is absorbed. Add
1$\frac{1}{2}$ l/3 pt/6 cups chicken stock or water with
half the saffron and liquid and plenty of salt
and pepper. Add the remaining ingredients
in the following order, pushing them well
down into the rice: browned chicken; squid,
if used; smoked ham; chorizo sausages;
tomatoes, white fish, and shrimps. Set the
mussels or clams on top. *Paella can be prepared 2 hours ahead up to this point.*

A half hour before serving: Bring the
liquid to the boil and boil fairly rapidly,
uncovered, on top of stove or outdoors on a
barbecue until all the liquid has been absorbed – this should take 18–20 minutes
and the rice will just be tender. Add more
water or stock if the liquid evaporates
before the rice is cooked. Turn the heat to
low and keep the paella warm for 5–10
minutes for the flavours to blend before
serving.

Flan

---

4 l/8 pt milk
2 tsp ground cinnamon
grated rind 2 lemons
24 eggs
450 g/1 lb/2 cups sugar

For caramel
700 g/1½ lb/3 cups sugar
5 dl/1 pt/2 cups water

3 plain moulds or soufflé dishes (2 1/4 pt capacity each)

This recipe can be doubled to bake in 6 moulds. If quantities are halved, use two 1½ l/3 pt moulds and reduce baking time to ¾–1 hour.

For the caramel: Heat the 700 g/1½ lb/3 cups sugar gently with the water until dissolved; bring to the boil and cook steadily to a rich brown caramel. *The caramel must be well browned or it will be unpleasantly sweet, but do not let it burn because it will turn bitter.* Immediately pour a third of the caramel into one of the moulds and turn the mould so the bottom and sides are coated with caramel. Repeat with the other two moulds, working as quickly as possible. If the caramel in the pan sets before the last mould is coated, melt it over gentle heat. Set the oven at moderate (180°C, Mark 4, 350°F).

Bring the milk to the boil and stir in the cinnamon and grated lemon rind. Beat the eggs with the 450 g/1 lb/2 cups sugar in a large bowl with a whisk until thick and light coloured, and stir in the hot milk. Strain this custard into the caramel-lined moulds, and cover tightly with foil, making sure the foil does not touch the custard. Set the moulds in roasting pans and add about 5 cm/2 inches hot water to make a bain marie. *To avoid bubbles arounds the edge of the cooked custard, the level of the water should come above the level of the custard in the dish.* Bring to the boil on top of the stove and bake the moulds in the heated oven for 1–1¼ hours or until a knife inserted in the centre comes out clean. Let the flans cool, covered, and keep them in the refrigerator. *You can prepare 24 hours ahead up to this point.*

A short time before serving, run the tip of a knife around the edge of each flan and unmould onto deep serving dishes (the caramel will form a small amount of sauce). Serve at room temperature.

MENUS
FOR FIFTY

A Formal Buffet

A Feast of Curry

Cocktail Party Canapés

Single-Plate Supper

MENUS FOR FIFTY

If in an unguarded moment you have blithely agreed to cook for a party of fifty, reflect before you commit yourself – this is a task usually undertaken only by professionals. But if your mind is set, you will find that entertaining large numbers has many rewards. For your guests, it will be a memorable occasion, whether the pretext for the party is an important anniversary or birthday, a reunion of old friends, or a fund-raising event. Entertaining in hired facilities just isn't the same, and though giving a party at home is time-consuming, your labour is free. You should inquire about case prices for wines and spirits to bring the bar cost down, and see if you can get a friendly meat or fish wholesaler to help out with the food budget. You will also find that cooking for large numbers is much quicker than making the same meal for fewer people several times over.

As commander of this culinary campaign, you should first review your resources: Do you have sufficient pots and pans, oven, stove top, and refrigerator space to make a meal for fifty? If not, can you borrow whatever is missing? To avoid last-minute shortages of linen, cutlery, glasses, and plates, you may do best to hire them from a catering firm.

Then consider your personnel. For a two-course buffet, where guests help themselves and sit at tables, you will need at least three waiters (one doubling as bartender) and two helpers in the kitchen to take care of last-minute cooking and the washing up. For a cocktail party or a stand-up meal, plan on two waiter-bartenders and someone to wash up.

Finally, having assessed what resources you can muster, you can decide on the kind of party – formal or informal, in or out of doors – that will suit the occasion best.

Handsome and hearty fare is to be found in the Formal Buffet. The main dish is a great platter of braised boeuf à la mode, shining with aspic, decorated with truffles, and garnished with colourful mounds of vegetables. Dessert brings a choice – a spectacular chocolate snowball, frosted all over with whipped cream, or trifle, a confection greater than its name suggests. All these dishes are cold, and preparation and serving are easy.

If you prefer hot buffet dishes, why not offer your friends a Feast of Curry. Four curries of totally different flavours are served with chutneys, dahl, and other appropriate condiments. Since such spiced dishes mellow if cooked a day or two in advance and aren't spoiled by reheating, they are ideal dishes to make ahead for large numbers. Curries are also ideal for serving outdoors; two other suitable outdoor meals will be found in Menus for Twenty-four. The Kebab Barbecue is an everybody-cooks meal and the Outdoor Lunch includes Spanish gazpacho and paella; both menus can be doubled easily.

When you want to serve more than cheese or nuts or olives with drinks, the menu for Cocktail Party Canapés is a feast in itself. The colourful array includes smoked salmon rolls, shrimp toasts, and stuffed tomatoes. Or for a taste of the Middle East, simply double the quantities in the Exotic Cocktail Party in Menus for Twenty-four.

The simplest party of all for large numbers is the Single-Plate Supper. The substantial snack of oxtail soup and finger foods needs a minimum of equipment for cooking and serving. This menu would be an excellent solution when catering for charity affairs or to take to a sports event because all the food is portable. All you need is a burner to reheat the soup; if there is an oven to warm the Cornish pasties, all well and good, but if not, they are just as good served cold.

A Formal Buffet

Boeuf â la Mode en Gelée

Canard à l'Orange en Gelée

Rice Salad or Potato Vinaigrette

Green Salad

Chocolate Snowball

Trifle

As usual, the French knew what they were doing when they developed the elaborate aspic-coated dishes that are the centrepiece of any grand buffet table. Not only do they make a stunning spectacle, glistening with glaze and abloom with garnishes, but the coating of aspic prevents drying out – a boon for the cook who must work ahead.

Both the boeuf à la mode and the canard à l'orange are typical of the dishes designed for such occasions. The beef is first braised with wine, veal bones, and pig's feet for richness. Then the cooking liquid is clarified with an egg white 'filter' to make a dark, gleaming aspic that, thanks to the veal bones, sets without benefit of added gelatine. The duck is simply roasted and the breast meat is carved and interleaved with orange segments before being coated with aspic flavoured with orange liqueur.

Aspic work is tricky until you get the knack of chilling until it is on the point of setting, then spooning it quickly over the cold food. Aspic at just the right – almost oily – consistency clings at once to cold food in a smooth, shiny layer. If you let the aspic get too cold, it will set before you have time to use it, but if you spoon over the aspic before it is at the setting point or before the food is ice-cold, it will simply run off into the bottom of the dish. Still, you can always start again by getting the aspic to the right temperature; a little practice will reward your patience.

Garnishes are an essential part of aspic dishes. Often they are so lavish, as in boeuf à la mode, that no other accompaniment is necessary. The sliced beef is surrounded by small piles or 'bouquets' of colourful vegetables – carrots, tomatoes, baby onions, and green beans – and the meat itself is decorated with contrasting designs of jet-black truffle and hard-boiled egg white. Naturally all this takes time, but at the end you will have a complete dish, so that the most you need add are a green salad (page 52) and the rice salad or potato vinaigrette (pages 91 and 164), increased to serve fifty people.

If the idea of dealing with a classic aspic makes you nervous or if you are short of time, boeuf à la mode can also be served in peasant style. Spoon a little of the strained cooking liquid over the meat, then leave it to jell. Chill the remaining cooking liquid in a tray until firmly set, then turn this sheet of aspic out onto damp greaseproof paper and chop it coarsely with a damp knife. Pile the chopped aspic around the platter of beef. Omit all the garnishes except for the bunches of watercress, but add more vegetables to the rice salad to make up the necessary quantity.

Duck with orange is quicker to prepare than the beef since the aspic recipe here calls for tinned consommé. When fortified with brandy and orange liqueur, this makes a well-flavoured aspic that will please most palates. This is not the time-consuming classic recipe for aspic, which would call for a well-flavoured homemade stock to be strained and clarified as in boeuf à la mode.

For dessert, nothing could be richer than chocolate snowball, and small servings are ample. It is a melting combination of sugar, butter, chocolate, and eggs – half fudge, half cake, that is unmoulded, coated with rosettes of whipped cream, and studded with candied violets.

Only slightly less rich is an old-English trifle. The name is doubtless ironic: cubes of sponge cake made into raspberry jam sandwiches and then soaked with sherry add up to more than a mere 'trifle'. Poached fruits, such as pears or peaches, are added, and the trifle is covered with a generous layer of vanilla custard. After letting the custard set and the flavours mellow in the wine for a day or two, top the trifle with whipped cream. Traditionally it is served in a cut-glass bowl.

A buffet of this magnitude obviously takes time to prepare, and you will need to start at least three days ahead with the chocolate snowball and the boeuf à la mode. However, as you will see from the timetable, there is almost nothing to be done on the day of the party; this frees you to handle the remaining arrangements.

COUNTDOWN

1–2 Weeks Before
Make chocolate snowball and cover.

2–3 Days Before
Braise boeuf à la mode and cover.
Roast ducks and keep covered.

1–2 Days Before
Clarify aspic for boeuf à la mode.
Make aspic for duck with orange.
Make trifle, but do not add cream; keep covered.
Make vinaigrette dressing for green salad and for potato or rice salad.

Day Before
Prepare garnishes for boeuf à la mode, slice beef, assemble platters, and coat with aspic; keep lightly covered.
Prepare orange segments for duck; carve ducks, coat with aspic and keep lightly covered.
For potato vinaigrette, cook potatoes and complete salad.
Or if making rice salad, cook rice and vegetables and keep separately, covered.
Wash salad greens and keep in plastic bags.

1–2 Hours Before Serving
Add watercress to boeuf à la mode and cover.
Cut orange garnish for duck and add to platter with watercress; cover.
Mix rice salad and keep at room temperature.
Put salad greens in bowls and cover.
Turn out chocolate snowball and decorate.
Decorate trifle.

Just Before Serving
Toss green salad.

Boeuf à la Mode en Gelée

4 beef joints (about 7 kg/16 lb) (e.g. sirloin,
    topside or silverside), larded and barded
2 pig's feet, washed and split
450 g/1 lb piece lean bacon, diced
10 medium onions, quartered
10 medium carrots, quartered
6 stalks celery, cut in 5-cm/2-inch sticks
2 bottles red wine
4 1/2 pt beef stock
6 cloves garlic, crushed
2 large bouquets garnis
24 peppercorns
salt
2 kg/4 lb veal bones

For garnish
3½ kg/8 lb baby or medium carrots
3½ kg/8 lb baby onions
2.75 kg/6 lb green beans, trimmed and cut
    in 5 cm/2 inch lengths
4 lb tomatoes, peeled
1 medium tin truffles, drained and liquid
    reserved
6 hard-boiled eggs
3 bunches watercress

For clarifying aspic
4 1/2 pt stock from cooking the beef
3.25 dl/¾ pt/1½ cups white wine
liquid reserved from canned truffles
2 dl/7 fl. oz/⅔ cup sherry
8 egg whites

Barding and larding (threading and covering the beef with pieces of pork fat) adds
richness to the meat. If your butcher won't
do it, turn to page 210. The flavour of beef
à la mode mellows if the meat is cooked 2–3
days ahead, However, once the aspic is
made and the meat is coated, the dish must
be served within 24 hours. By itself, this
quantity serves twenty-four to thirty people
and you can easily halve the recipe.

Two to three days ahead: Blanch the pig's
feet in boiling salted water 5 minutes and
drain. Set oven at moderately low (170°C,
Mark 3, 325°F).

To braise the beef: In two large casseroles fry
the bacon until browned. Lift out with a
slotted spoon and brown the beef well on all
sides. Take out, add the onions, carrots, and
celery, and cook gently until beginning to
brown. Replace the beef and the bacon and
add the wine, stock, garlic, bouquets garnis,
peppercorns, and a little salt. Tuck the
bones and pig's feet down beside the meat,
cover the pans, and bring to the boil. Braise
in the heated oven for 3–3½ hours or until
the meat is tender when pierced with a
skewer.

Let cool to tepid, then drain the meat,
wrap it in foil and chill. Strain the cooking
liquid, pressing well to extract all the juices,
and chill also. *You can prepare 2–3 days
ahead up to this point.*

The day before serving, cook the garnish: Peel
and quarter medium carrots, trimming
edges to form miniature carrots; scrub or
peel baby carrots, leaving on a little of the
green tops. Cook the carrots in boiling

salted water for 15–20 minutes or until tender and drain them.

Blanch the onions in boiling water for 1 minute, drain and peel them – the skins will strip away easily. Trim the roots and stems of the onions carefully so they will not fall apart during cooking. Cook the onions in boiling salted water for 10–15 minutes or until tender; drain and sprinkle with a little sugar.

Cook the beans in boiling salted water for 8–10 minutes until just tender, drain, rinse with cold water, and drain again. Chill all the vegetables and tomatoes.

The aspic must be made in two batches because there is too much liquid to clarify at once. When taken from the refrigerator, the stock (cooking liquid) to make the aspic should be firmly jelled if you have used plenty of pig's feet and veal bones. If not, gelatine must be added. Prepare it by sprinkling 15–20 g/$\frac{1}{2}$–$\frac{3}{4}$ oz/2–3 envelopes of gelatine (depending on how well set the cooking liquid is) over 1.75 dl/6 fl. oz/$\frac{3}{4}$ cup water in a small pan and let stand until spongy.

To make one batch of aspic: Skim all the fat from the surface of the stock. In a large pan put 2 litres/4 pints of the stock, add 1.45 dl/6 fl. oz/$\frac{3}{4}$ cup of wine and 6 tablespoons of sherry, and half the truffle liquid. Heat until the stock melts then taste for seasoning – aspic must be highly seasoned. *Salt and pepper cannot be added after the aspic is clarified because they make it cloudy.* If using gelatine, add half the softened gelatine to the stock at this point.

Add 4 egg whites and beat with a balloon whisk until the mixture froths slightly. Set the pan over medium heat and bring it to the boil, taking 10–15 minutes and beating constantly. *Be sure to whisk deep down into the mixture.*

As soon as the mixture boils, stop whisking and let the frothy filter of egg white on top of the liquid rise to the top of the pan. Take from the heat and let cool 5 minutes. Repeat the boiling and cooling procedure twice more, without whisking. Any liquid that bubbles through the filter should be crystal clear, but if not, repeat the boiling and rising once more.

Lay a scalded dish towel over a bowl and ladle the clarified aspic into it, sliding out the filter in one piece, if possible. The aspic that drains through the cloth should be clear and sparkling, but if not, strain it again through the filter and cloth. Lift the cloth, tie the ends together carefully without squeezing, and hang it from a bench or door handle until all the aspic has drained. Let it cool. Clarify the remaining cooking liquid in the same way and mix the two batches. *You can prepare 1–2 days ahead up to this point.* Keep the aspic, covered, in the refrigerator.

To assemble the dish: Discard outer fat and string from the meat and carve it in 1-cm/$\frac{3}{8}$-inch slices. Arrange the slices, overlapping slightly, on 3–4 large silver platters or deep trays. Chill thoroughly.

For decoration: Cut the truffles and the whites of the hard-boiled eggs in thin slices and cut out shapes – circles, crescents, diamonds, triangles, etc. Use a small knife and a plain piping nozzle or a sharp bottle top for circles and crescents. Dip the shapes in a saucer of liquid aspic and arrange them in a pattern on the meat. The aspic will make the design stick. One attractive design is the fleur de lys made with two crescents set on each side of a diamond.

To coat with aspic: When the aspic is cool, pour about 1 pt/2 cups into a metal bowl and set it over another bowl filled with ice. Stir it very gently with a large metal spoon until the consistency is oily (vigorous stirring makes the aspic bubbly) and it is about to set. *It sets quickly, so you must work fast.* Spoon a coating of aspic over the beef and chill again. If the aspic or the beef are not cold enough, the liquid will run into the bottom of the platter; do not continue, but chill aspic and meat to the right temperature. If the aspic is too cold and sets before you can use it, melt it and chill again.

Melt any solidified aspic in the bowl and add more to it; repeat the coating process with the other platter.

Arrange the chilled vegetables in eight neat piles down each side of the meat, leaving the ends of the platters empty. Coat the vegetables also with aspic and chill. Give both platters a final coating of aspic over both meat and vegetables and chill 1–2 hours.

You can prepare 24 hours ahead of serving up to this point. Keep the platters loosely covered with plastic wrap, in the refrigerator. *Do not let them get too cold or the aspic will crystallize.*

Just before serving, garnish the ends of each platter with a bouquet of watercress.

Canard à l'Orange en Gelée

8 ducks (2–2½ kg/4–5 lbs each)
salt and freshly ground black pepper
20 navel oranges

For aspic
35 g/1¼ oz/5 envelopes gelatine
10 tins (275 g/10½ oz each) beef consommé
1.25 dl/¼ pt/½ cup brandy
1.25 dl/¼ pt/½ cup Curaçao or other orange liqueur

For garnish
4 bunches watercress
6 navel oranges

trussing needle and string

It is important to use navel oranges in this recipe because they have no seeds. The recipe, served alone, is enough for between twenty-four and thirty people. Quantities can be halved or quartered.

Set the oven at hot (200°C, Mark 6, 400°F). Truss the ducks, sprinkle them with salt and pepper, and prick the skin to release the fat. Set them on one side on racks in roasting pans. Roast the ducks in the heated oven (if you have only one oven you will need to cook them in two batches) for 1½–1¾ hours or until the skin is crisp and brown and the thigh of the bird is tender when pierced with a fork. Turn the birds from one side to the other and finally onto their backs during cooking and baste them from time to time. Discard the fat as it collects in the base of the pan. Let the ducks cool, then cover and chill them.

For the aspic: Sprinkle the gelatine over 2 tins of the consommé in a pan and let stand 5–10 minutes until spongy. Melt over gentle heat and stir into the remaining consommé with the brandy and orange liqueur. *You can prepare 1–2 days ahead up to this point.* Keep the aspic, covered, in the refrigerator.

To segment the oranges: Cut the peel and pith from the 20 oranges, using a serrated-edged knife, and cut with a sawing motion around the orange as when peeling an apple. Cut down on each side of the segments of orange and scoop them out, folding back the skin that is left like the pages of a book.

To carve the ducks: Discard the trussing strings and cut the skin between the leg and breast of the bird, but do not remove the leg. Cut along the top of the breastbone and work down one side toward the wing bone, cutting the breast meat from the bone in one piece but leaving the breastbone attached to the rest of the duck. When all the breast meat is loose, cut it free at the bottom, leaving the wing bone attached to the bird. Repeat on the other side of the duck. Cut each breast into 4–5 diagonal slices.

To assemble the dish: Replace the breast meat on the duck carcasses, with a segment of orange between each slice. Set the ducks on platters, drain the remaining orange segments, and pile them on the platters beside the ducks. Chill very thoroughly.

To coat with aspic: If the aspic has set, melt it; spoon 5 dl/1 pt/2 cups into a metal bowl. Set the bowl over another bowl of ice and stir the aspic very gently with a large metal spoon until the consistency is oily and it is about to set (vigorous stirring makes the aspic bubbly). *It sets quickly, so work fast.* Spoon a coating over the ducks and chill them again. If the aspic or the duck are not cold enough, the liquid will run into the bottom of the platter. Do not continue, but chill aspic and duck to the right temperature. If the aspic is too cold and sets before you can use it, melt it and chill again.

Melt any solidified aspic in the bowl and repeat the coating process until all the ducks are completely covered with aspic. When adding the last coating, spoon some aspic onto the orange segments and the base of the platters. Keep loosely covered with plastic wrap, in the refrigerator. *Do not let them get too cold or the aspic will crystallize. You can prepare 24 hours ahead up to this point.*

For decoration: If possible, use an orange rind cutter to remove strips of peel from the oranges, working from top to bottom. Cut the oranges in half from top to bottom, then cut crosswise into semicircular slices – each slice will be indented with 'teeth'.

A short time before serving, arrange the orange slices around the edge of the platter and garnish the dish with watercress. Serve the breast meat of the ducks first, then remove the legs, discard the duck carcasses, and arrange the legs on one platter for second helpings.

Chocolate Snowball

1 kg/2 lb sweet chocolate
3.25 dl/$\frac{3}{4}$ pt/1$\frac{1}{2}$ cups strong black coffee
1 kg/2 lb/4 cups unsalted butter
1 kg/2 lb/4 cups sugar
16 eggs

For decoration
1.25 dl/$\frac{1}{4}$ pt/$\frac{1}{2}$ cup brandy
3 tbs sugar
1$\frac{1}{2}$ l/3 pt/6 cups double cream, stiffly
   whipped
box candied violets

*3 charlotte moulds or deep metal bowls (1$\frac{1}{2}$-l/
3-pt/6-cup capacity each); icing bag medium
star nozzle*

You can easily halve or quarter this recipe.
This quantity serves twenty-four to thirty
people.

Line the moulds or bowls with a double
thickness of foil. Set the oven at moderate
(180°C, Mark 4, 350°F).

The mixture must be made in two parts
because the full amount is too difficult to
stir. In a heavy-based pan melt 450 g/1 lb
chocolate in 1.8 dl/6 fl. oz/$\frac{3}{4}$ cup coffee over
low heat, stirring until the chocolate melts.
Cook, stirring, until the mixture almost
holds its shape. Add 450 g/1 lb/2 cups
butter and 450 g/1 lb/2 cups sugar, a little
at a time, stirring until dissolved. Heat until
very hot, but do not boil. Take from the
heat and beat in 8 eggs, one by one. The
heat of the mixture will thicken the eggs.
Strain the mixture into the prepared
moulds, filling one completely and another
half full. Make the remaining mixture in the
same way and fill all the moulds.

Bake them in the heated oven for 50–60
minutes or until a thick crust has formed
on top. The mixture will rise slightly but
will fall again as it cools. Let cool, then
cover and keep at least 3 days or up to 2
weeks in the refrigerator.

Not more than 3 hours before serving:
Run a knife around the moulds and turn
them out onto serving dishes. Peel off the
foil – the mixture tends to stick and may
look messy. Beat the brandy and sugar into
the whipped cream, put a third to half of
this cream in an icing bag fitted with a star
nozzle and pipe rosettes all over the moulds,
covering the chocolate mixture completely;
do not use too much cream at once because
it is hard to handle. Fill the icing bag with
more cream as necessary. Top the centre of
each snowball with a single large rosette.
Stud the top and sides with candied violets;
chill until serving.

Trifle

---

1 kg/2 lb pound cake, sponge cake, or angel food cake
1 jar (350 g/12 oz) raspberry jam
2.5 dl/½ pt/1 cup sherry
2 tins (1½ kg/2 lb each) sliced pears or peaches, drained
50 g/2 oz/½ cup whole blanched almonds
5 dl/1 pt/2 cups double cream, stiffly whipped

For the custard
1½ l/3 pt milk
2 vanilla pods, split, or 3 tsp vanilla extract
8 eggs
10 egg yolks
350 g/¾ lb/1½ cups sugar

2 glass bowls (about 3 l/6 pt capacity each); icing bag and medium star nozzle

This recipe can be halved – the above quantity serves twenty-four to thirty.

Cut the cake in thirds horizontally and sandwich it with the raspberry jam; cut it in 2½-cm/1-inch squares. Put the squares in the bottom of the bowls and spoon in sherry; press down lightly. Add drained fruit.

For the custard: Scald the milk with the vanilla pod and leave in a warm place to infuse for 10–15 minutes. Do not add vanilla extract at this point. Beat the eggs and egg yolks with the sugar until light and fairly thick. Stir in half the hot milk and stir this mixture back into the remaining milk. Heat gently, stirring constantly, until the custard thickens slightly; if you draw your finger across the back of the spoon, it will leave a clear trail. *Do not overcook or boil or the custard will curdle.* Some cooks like to make custard in a double boiler to insure that it will not get too hot. Take the custard at once from the heat and strain it into a bowl (the vanilla pod can be washed, dried, and used again). If using vanilla extract, add it now. Sprinkle lightly with sugar to prevent a skin from forming and let cool to tepid. Pour the custard over the cake and fruit – they should be completely covered. Cover and chill. For decoration: Toast the almonds in a moderate oven (180°C, Mark 4, 350°F) for 8–10 minutes or until browned. *You can prepare 48 hours ahead up to this point.* Keep trifle, covered, in refrigerator.

Not more than 3 hours before serving, put the whipped cream into an icing bag fitted with a star nozzle and cover the custard completely with small rosettes of cream. Alternatively make a lattice of cream so the custard shows through, and pipe rosettes around the edge of the bowl. Top the rosettes with browned almonds.

A Feast of Curry

Mild Chicken Curry

Hot Lamb Curry

Shrimp Curry

Meatball Curry

Dahl

Mango Chutney

Fresh Date and Ginger
Chutney

Poppadums

Tomato and Cucumber
Raita

Aubergine Bhartha

Boiled Rice

Macédoine of Tropical
Fruits

The very idea of an Indian feast evokes images of grand palaces, bejewelled potentates, and tray after tray of exotic, highly spiced food. The palaces and potentates may have disappeared from the scene, but the cooking can be re-created with remarkably little effort and is an exotic way of feeding large numbers.

Spices are the key. In Tamil, the oldest language of southern India, the word 'kari' means sauce, and correctly curry refers not to a single spice but to any spiced dish with a sauce. The curry powder we know is simply a convenient blend of spices. An Indian cook mixes his own spices and often grinds them freshly as well, varying the combinations and using a dozen or more in a single dish.

Spices commonly used to make curries are coriander, cumin, cardamom, cloves, cinnamon, saffron, nutmeg, mace, mustard, and aniseed. Often turmeric is included for colour and flavour, with chili for hotness, and fresh ginger to temper the heat. Garlic and onions help 'marry' the mixture, and in southern India, milk made from grated coconut is a favourite ingredient. All these elements of a curry are carefully blended, then cooked long and slowly to develop the flavours. Since an extra hour's cooking rarely affects quality, curries are the ideal dish to make ahead and reheat for large numbers, particularly since they mellow if kept for a day or two.

At a banquet, curries of several flavours and degrees of heat are served at once, like those suggested in this menu. In India they would all probably be much hotter than here, and you can vary the heat to your

185

taste by adjusting the amount of red chili pepper.

As important as the balance of spices is the balance of dishes that accompany the curries. They should vary both in texture and taste. Dahl is a smooth neutral purée made of dried beans or lentils. Raita, based on a curd very like yogurt, adds a cooling touch. Several chutneys, hot or mild, fresh or pickled, are mandatory. Mango chutney is one of the few available commercially, so do use it in this menu, and also make fresh date and ginger chutney. Of the many kinds of Indian bread, poppadums are sold in most Oriental stores or good grocers. They are thin wafers in varying flavours, which are baked till crisp or deep fried and then crumbled over the curry.

In India, each guest is given a tray with the curries and accompaniments in small bowls, with bread or a mound of rice in the centre. In the West, the simplest way to serve curry is to set out the dishes on a long buffet table and leave guests to serve themselves, starting with the rice. All the hot dishes – curries, rice, and dahl – can be kept warm almost indefinitely on table burners. Beer is the best accompaniment.

Desserts are not customary after curry in India. The usual ending to a meal is 'paan' – a leaf filled with betel nut and spices to be chewed as a digestive – or fresh fruit. An excellent ending to a Western-style curry feast would be a macédoine of such tropical fruits as papaya, melon, pineapple, banana, and mango. The more fresh fruit you use the better, though a few tinned ones can be included.

COUNTDOWN

In this countdown, an hour is allowed
for reheating the curries, although the
required heating time may not be as
long; it depends on the size of the pan.
When the curries are hot, transfer them
to a roasting pan of boiling water on top
of the stove (a bain marie) or keep them
warm on table burners.

2–3 Days Before
Make chicken curry, but do not add
    spring onions and lime juice; cover.
Make lamb curry and cover.
Make curried meatballs and cover.

2 Days Before
Make shrimp curry, but do not add
    coriander and red chili pepper; cover.
Make dahl, but do not add fried onions;
    cover.
Make date and ginger chutney and keep
    tightly covered.
Make aubergine bhartha and cover.

Day Before
Make raita and cover; do not add
    coriander.
Cook rice, spread in buttered baking
    dishes, and cover with foil.

In the Morning
Chop spring onions and squeeze lime
    juice for chicken curry.
Chop coriander for shrimp curry and for
    raita.
Fry onions for dahl and drain.

Bake or fry poppadums and keep tightly
    covered at room temperature.
Make fruit macédoine and keep tightly
    covered.

3–4 Hours Before Serving
Pile mango chutney and date and ginger
    chutney in bowls and cover.
Put aubergine bhartha in bowls and
    cover.
Pile raita in bowls, sprinkle with corian-
    der, and cover.

1½ Hours Before Serving
Set oven at moderate (180°C, Mark 4,
    350°F).

1 Hour Before Serving
Reheat all four curries on top of stove or
    in oven.
Reheat dahl.

30 Minutes Before Serving
Reheat rice in oven.
Pile poppadums on a tray.

15 Minutes Before Serving
Take chutneys, poppadums, raita, and
    bhartha to the table.
Stir spring onions and lime juice into
    chicken curry and taste for seasoning.
Sprinkle shrimp curry with coriander and
    red chili pepper.
Sprinkle shrimp over dahl.

Mild Chicken Curry

1.75 dl/6 fl. oz/¾ cup oil
6 chickens (1–2 kg/3–3½ lb each), cut in 8
  pieces
12 large onions, chopped
9 cloves garlic, crushed
1½ tbs ground coriander
1½ tbs freshly ground black pepper
1½ tbs ground allspice
1 tbs ground cloves
1 tbs ground turmeric
seeds from 4 cardamom pods, crushed
1½–2 l/3–3½ pt/6–7 cups stock
2 tsp salt
12 spring onions, chopped
juice of 3 limes

If served alone, this recipe is enough for
twenty to twenty-four people; it is easy to
divide in half or thirds.

In 1 large or 2 medium casseroles, heat half
the oil and sauté the chicken pieces, a few
at a time, until browned on all sides. Take
them out, add the onions and garlic and
cook slowly until golden brown. Take them
out, add the remaining oil and stir in the
coriander, black pepper, and allspice, cloves,
turmeric, and cardamom seeds. Cook very
slowly, stirring, for 2 minutes. *Do not let the
spices burn.* Replace the onions and garlic,
stir well, and cook gently 2 minutes longer.

   Add 1½ l/3 pt/6 cups stock to the pan
with the salt; stir and replace the chicken
pieces. Baste the chicken with the curry
mixture, cover, bring to the boil, and
simmer 30–35 minutes or until the chicken
is very tender, adding more stock if the
mixture gets dry. Taste the sauce, adding
more salt and pepper if needed. Let cool,
then keep in the refrigerator for 2–3 days
for the flavours to mellow.

   To serve: Reheat the chicken in a moderate oven (180°C, Mark 4, 350°F), allowing
25–30 minutes for the smaller casserole or
45–50 minutes for the large one, or reheat
gently on top of the stove until very hot.
Stir in the spring onions and lime juice.
Serve in the casseroles.

Coconut Milk

7.5 dl/1½ pt/3 cups boiling water
350 g/¾ lb/3 cups grated fresh coconut or
  350 g/¾ lb/3 cups dried unsweetened
  coconut

This quantity gives about 7.5 dl/1½ pt/3
cups milk and you can easily make more or
less.

Pour the boiling water over the coconut
and let stand 30 minutes. Drain through
cheesecloth, squeezing tightly to extract all
the milk.

Hot Lamb Curry

1.75 dl/6 fl. oz/¾ cup oil
3½ kg/8 lb boneless leg or lean shoulder of
    lamb, cut in 4-cm/1½-inch cubes
8 medium onions, chopped
6 tbs ground coriander
2 tbs ground cumin
1–1½ tbs ground red chili pepper, or to taste
2 tsp ground cinnamon
1 tsp ground nutmeg
coconut milk made with 350 g/¾ lb/3 cups
    coconut (see previous recipe)
1 tsp salt
12 (2 kg/4 lb) tomatoes, peeled, seeded, and
    coarsely chopped or 2 tins (1 kg/2 lb
    each) tomatoes, drained and coarsely
    chopped

You can halve or quarter this recipe – by
itself the full amount serves twelve to fifteen
people.

In 1 large or 2 medium casseroles, heat half
the oil and sauté the cubes of lamb, a few
at a time, until browned on all sides. Take
them out, add the onions and cook slowly
until golden brown. Take them out, add the
remaining oil and stir in the coriander,
cumin, chili pepper, cinnamon, and nutmeg. Cook very slowly, stirring, for 2–3
minutes. *Do not let the spices burn.* Replace
the onions, stir well, and cook gently 2
minutes longer.

Add coconut milk to the pan with the
salt. Replace the meat, stir to mix, cover
and bring to the boil. Simmer 1½–2 hours,
stirring occasionally, or until the meat is
tender. Stir in the tomatoes and continue
cooking 10 minutes longer. Taste the sauce
for seasoning, adding more salt or ground
red chili pepper if liked. Let cool, then keep
the curry in the refrigerator for 2–3 days for
the flavours to mellow.

To serve: Reheat the lamb in a moderate
oven (180°C, Mark 4, 350°F), allowing
25–30 minutes for the smaller casseroles or
45–50 minutes for the large one, or reheat
gently on top of the stove until very hot.
Serve the curry in the casserole.

Shrimp Curry

2.7 kg/6 lb uncooked medium shrimps,
  peeled
3.25 dl/$\frac{3}{4}$ pt/1$\frac{1}{2}$ cups oil
6 onions, thinly sliced
6 tbs chopped fresh ginger root
6 tbs ground coriander
2 tbs ground cumin
1 tbs ground turmeric
1$\frac{1}{2}$ tsp ground nutmeg
1$\frac{1}{2}$ tsp celery seed
1 tsp salt
coconut milk made with 450 g/1 lb/4$\frac{1}{2}$ cups
  coconut (see page 188)
6 tbs lemon juice

To finish
1 tbs chopped fresh coriander (optional)
$\frac{1}{2}$ tsp ground red chili pepper (optional)

This recipe is easy to halve or quarter; the
full quantity serves from twelve to fifteen
people. Fresh coriander, also called cilantro
or Italian parsley, is sold in Latin American
and Oriental groceries.

In 1 large casserole or 2 large frying pans
heat half the oil and sauté the shrimps a
few at a time over fairly high heat for 1–2
minutes until they begin to turn pink. Add
more oil as necessary, reserving 2 tablespoons. Take them out, heat 1 tablespoon
oil in each pan, and add the onions and
chopped ginger; cook over medium heat
until golden brown. Add the ground coriander, cumin, turmeric, nutmeg, celery seed,
and salt and continue cooking 2 minutes,
stirring. *Do not let the spices burn.* Add the
coconut milk, replace the shrimps and simmer 5 minutes. Sprinkle with lemon juice
and taste for seasoning. *You can prepare 2
days ahead up to this point.* If preparing
ahead, simmer the shrimps for 2 instead of
5 minutes and keep, covered, in the refrigerator. Reheat for 10–15 minutes on top of
the stove until very hot.

To serve: Transfer the shrimps to a
serving bowl, or leave them in the casserole. Sprinkle with fresh coriander and red
chili pepper if you like.

Meatball Curry

For the meatballs
2¾ kg / 6 lb minced lamb or beef
1 fresh green chili or 1 tinned chili
3 cloves garlic, crushed
2 tbs / ½ cup chopped fresh coriander (see
    previous recipe)
3 tbs ground coriander
1 tbs ground cinnamon
1 tbs ground cumin
1 tsp ground cloves
1 tsp ground mace or nutmeg
1 tsp salt
3.25 dl / ¾ pt / 1½ cups plain yogurt
3 eggs, beaten to mix

For the sauce
6 tbs oil
3 onions, thinly sliced
3 tomatoes, peeled, seeded, and chopped, or
    450 g / 1 lb / 2 cups canned tomatoes,
    drained and chopped
3 tbs (35 g / 1½ oz) chopped fresh ginger root
1½ tbs ground turmeric
1½ tbs ground cumin
3 cloves garlic, crushed
1 tsp ground red chili pepper
7.5 dl / 1½ pt / 3 cups plain yogurt
7.5 dl / 1½ pt / 3 cups hot water
1 tsp salt
6 tbs / ½ cup chopped fresh coriander (see
    previous recipe)

If you prefer a mild curry, omit the red chili pepper. You can easily divide the quantities in thirds – the full amount serves from twelve to fifteen.

Core, seed, and chop the fresh chili or drain, rinse, and chop the tinned chili. *Handle fresh chilies with gloves as the oil can burn your skin.*

To make the meatballs: Mix the meat, fresh or tinned chili, garlic, fresh and ground coriander, cinnamon, cumin, cloves and mace or nutmeg with salt and work twice through the fine plate of a mincer. Work in the yogurt with enough beaten egg to bind the mixture and taste it for seasoning. Dampen your hands and roll the mixture into 4-cm / 1½-inch balls.

For the sauce: In 2 large pans heat the oil and sauté the onions until golden brown. Add the tomatoes, ginger root, turmeric, cumin, garlic, and red chili pepper and cook gently, stirring, for 2–3 minutes. Add the yogurt and simmer 10 minutes. Stir in the hot water and salt, carefully add the meatballs, and sprinkle the chopped coriander on top. Simmer, uncovered, for 30 minutes or until the meatballs are no longer pink in the centre. Taste the sauce for seasoning. Cover and let cool, then keep in the refrigerator for 2–3 days for the flavour to mellow.

   To serve: Reheat the meatballs, covered, in a moderate oven (180°C, Mark 4, 350°F) for 20–25 minutes or heat gently on top of the stove until very hot. Transfer to a dish for serving.

Dahl

1½ kg/3½ lb/8 cups lentils
3 l/6 pt beef or chicken stock
3–3½ l/6–7 pt water
1 tbs turmeric
2 tbs ground coriander
1 tbs ground cinnamon
1 tbs ground cumin
1 tsp ground cloves
1 tsp ground nutmeg
1 tsp salt

To finish
1.80 dl/6 fl oz/¾ cup oil
8 onions, thinly sliced

For reheating, you will find it easier to put the dahl into 2 or 3 pans instead of 1 large one. The recipe can be halved or quartered.

Soak the lentils overnight in water to cover. Drain them and put them in a large pan with the stock, 3 l/6 pt water, and turmeric. Bring to the boil, cover and simmer 1–1½ hours until the lentils are very soft. Drain and reserve any liquid and work the lentils through a food mill or purée them, a little at a time, in a blender. Add the coriander, cinnamon, cumin, cloves, nutmeg, and salt, and beat with a spoon, adding enough of the reserved cooking liquid to make the consistency soft and smooth, not sticky or soupy. Taste the dahl for seasoning.

For the garnish: Heat the oil and fry the onions until thoroughly browned; drain them on paper towels. *You can prepare 48 hours ahead up to this point.* Keep dahl and onions, covered, separately in the refrigerator.

If preparing ahead, reheat the dahl in a moderate oven (180°C, Mark 4, 350°F), allowing 20–25 minutes for smaller casseroles, or 35–45 minutes for large ones, or reheat gently on top of the stove until very hot. Reheat the fried onions on top of the stove.

Serve in the casserole or transfer to a bowl and sprinkle with the fried onions.

Fresh Date and Ginger Chutney

75 g/3 oz/1 cup peeled pieces fresh ginger
   root
1.25 dl/¼ pt/½ cup lemon juice
4 onions, cut in pieces
6 cloves garlic, crushed
100 g/¼ lb/1 cup chopped stoned dates
125 g/5 oz/1 cup sultanas
½–1 tsp salt

This recipe makes about 1 kg/2 lb/4 cups chutney and you can halve or increase the quantities.

Purée the ginger, lemon juice, onions, garlic, dates, sultanas, and salt in a blender, a little at a time. Transfer to a bowl. Mix thoroughly and taste for seasoning. The chutney can be kept, tightly covered, in the refrigerator for up to 2 days, and the flavour will mellow.

Tomato and Cucumber Raita

10 cucumbers
salt
10 tomatoes, peeled, seeded, and chopped
  (see page 207)
4 onions, finely chopped
2½ l/5 pt/10 cups plain yogurt
6 tbs chopped fresh coriander (page 190) –
  for sprinkling

Served on its own, raita is an unusual appetizer – this quantity gives about 3 quarts, but you can easily make less.

Peel the cucumbers, cut them in half lengthwise, and scoop out the seeds with a teaspoon. Shred the cucumbers on a coarse grater, sprinkle lightly with salt, and leave in a colander, topped with a plate and a weight, for about 1 hour. Press to extract the bitter juices and mix with the tomatoes, onions, yogurt, and more salt if needed. *You can prepare 24 hours ahead up to this point.* Keep the raita tightly covered in the refrigerator.

To serve: Pile in a bowl and sprinkle with chopped fresh coriander.

Eggplant Bhartha

8 large aubergines
1.25 dl/¼ pt/½ cup oil
10 fresh or tinned green chilies
2 onions, very finely chopped
2 tbs ground cumin
juice of 2 lemons
1 tsp salt

Aubergine, or eggplant, bhartha makes a good cocktail dip, resembling poor man's caviar (page 158) but with a very hot flavour. This quantity makes about 1 kg/2 lb/4 cups and the recipe can easily be halved.

Set oven at moderate (180°C, Mark 4, 350°F).

Trim ends of aubergines and rub the skins with the oil. Bake them in the heated oven for 1 hour or until soft. Let cool slightly, then peel off the skin and discard; mash the flesh. Core, seed, and very finely chop fresh chilies or drain, rinse, and very finely chop tinned chilies. *Handle fresh chilies with gloves because the oil can burn your hands.*

Stir the chilies, onions, cumin, lemon juice, and salt into the aubergine flesh. You can make the bhartha up to 48 hours ahead. Taste for seasoning and keep it, covered, in the refrigerator.

Poppadums

Poppadums are thin round wafers about 15 cm/6 inches in diameter before cooking. You will find several kinds – spicy, coloured, and plain – in most Oriental stores. Allow 2 poppadums per person.

To cook them: Bake in a hot oven (200°C, Mark 6, 400°F) for 3–4 minutes or until puffed and brown. Alternatively, fry them in hot deep fat, holding them down with a spatula, for 10 seconds or until puffed and brown; then drain on paper towels.

Boiled Rice

For fifty people you will need about 2.75 kg/ 6 lb/12 cups of rice (200 g/$\frac{1}{2}$ lb/1 cup is enough for four people). Cook the rice in 3–4 batches in plenty of boiling water for 10–12 minutes or until just tender. Drain in a colander and rinse with hot water to wash away the starch. Poke a few drainage holes with the handle of a spoon and let the rice dry 15–20 minutes. Spread it in a layer not more than 5 cm/2 inches deep in buttered roasting pans or baking dishes and cover with buttered foil. *You can prepare 24 hours ahead up to this point.* Keep the rice in the refrigerator.

Reheat the rice in a moderate oven (180°C, Mark 4, 350°F) for 15–20 minutes or until very hot. Remove the foil, stir the rice with a fork, and replace in the oven for 2–3 minutes to dry. Pile in a serving dish and sprinkle generously with paprika.

Macédoine of Tropical Fruits

3 ripe medium papayas, seeds discarded and flesh scooped into balls
3 medium ripe melons, seeds discarded and flesh scooped into balls
8 bananas, peeled and cut in diagonal slices
3 fresh pineapples, peeled, cored and cut in chunks (page 207)
6–8 mangoes, peeled and sliced, discarding the seeds
6–8 passion fruits (optional)
450 g/1 lb tinned lichees
450 g/1 lb tinned figs
juice 5 lemons
1–1$\frac{1}{4}$ kg/2–2$\frac{1}{2}$ lb/4–5 cups sugar (or to taste)

Passion fruit adds inimitable flavour to a macédoine, but some people do not like the seeds. You can substitute tinned for many of the fresh fruits, but the flavour will not be as good. The amount of sugar you need depends on the tartness of the fruits – if most is tinned, no extra sugar will be necessary. You can easily halve these quantities or, to decrease them still further, omit some of the fruits.

If using passion fruits, cut off the tops and scoop out pulp and seeds with a teaspoon, discarding the shells. Drain canned fruits, reserving the syrup.

Arrange all the fruits in layers in glass bowls, sprinkling each layer with lemon juice and a little sugar. Spoon over the reserved syrup and sprinkle the top fruits with sugar to discourage browning. Cover tightly and chill at least 6 and up to 24 hours.

Cocktail Party Canapés

COLD HORS D'OEUVRE

Assorted Cheese Pastries
Smoked Salmon Rolls
Stuffed Tomatoes

HOT HORS D'OEUVRE

Devils and Angels on Horseback
Shrimp Toasts
Cheese Dreams

The best canapés have several common denominators. They look good, with clear flavours that can compete with the most potent cocktail, and they are easy to eat in one, or at most two, bites. They are robust enough to resist the heat of the average party and strong enough to survive a clumsy snatch from the dish – nothing is more irritating than a canapé that collapses at a touch.

Finding canapés to meet these criteria is not as difficult as it might seem, and out of consideration for the host who is also cook, all the cold hors d'oeuvre in this menu can be made well in advance. Indeed the cheese pastry can be made and filled weeks ahead since it freezes perfectly. The pastry itself is deliciously rich and crumbly and you can add all manner of fillings. Anchovies, sausage, and cheese are suggested here, but chopped ham, chopped cooked chicken livers, or stuffed olives would be equally good, shaped as for the sausage rolls. Be sure to make the dough fast and to chill it thoroughly before rolling it out; otherwise it will become sticky and unmanageable.

Smoked salmon rolls are at their best when made with wafer-thin slices of bread (cut from an unsliced loaf) and with very finely sliced smoked salmon. If it is cut too thick, the rolls are clumsy. Tiny tomatoes alternately stuffed with cream cheese and with caviar will make a cheerful checkerboard pattern when arranged on the platter.

Hot hors d'oeuvre are less easy to organize in advance. However, the picturesquely named devils and angels on horseback can be assembled well ahead of the party, and a few minutes' wait in the oven after cooking won't harm them. They are bacon rolls filled with chicken livers or stoned prunes (for devils) and oysters (for angels). In this recipe they have lost their horses of toast, but you can remount them if you like.

Both the shrimp toasts – familiar as an appetizer in Chinese restaurants – and the cheese dreams are less accommodating. While quick to prepare, they must be fried in deep fat and served at once while still crisp. If you don't have someone in the kitchen to take charge of this, you will do best to omit them and make double the quantity of devils and angels on horseback.

How many canapés you need to serve fifty guests will depend on their appetites and their plans for the rest of the evening. If everyone is going on to dinner, they will probably eat less, but if you have a high proportion of young people, plan on extras. The quantities in this menu amount to 8 canapés per person or 400 for fifty guests. This sounds like a lot, but by spreading the work out over several days you will still be unflustered on the day of the party.

The traditional way to serve hors d'oeuvres is on a silver platter or tray filled with serried rows of canapés, each of a different kind. Parsley sprigs are invaluable for adding colour as garnish. Caterers will be happy to hire out silver or stainless steel trays and platters at the same time as glasses, ice buckets and other cocktail party paraphernalia. For cold canapés, the trays are usually left plain, but for hot canapés, particularly greasy ones, the tray should be lined with a linen napkin. Be sure the platters are kept filled and circulate freely during the party. This insures both that the hot canapés come straight from the kitchen and that guests don't bunch in awkward knots around one table.

COUNTDOWN

1–2 Days Before
Make and bake cheese pastries and store in an airtight container, layered with greaseproof paper.

1 Day Ahead
Make smoked salmon rolls and wrap tightly.
Make mixture for cheese balls and cover.

In the Morning
Fill tomatoes, chill, then cover.
Prepare devils and angels on horseback but do not cook; cover.
Make shrimp toasts, but do not fry; cover.

2–3 Hours Before Serving
Arrange cheese pastries on trays; keep covered at room temperature.
Arrange salmon rolls on platters; keep covered at room temperature.
Arrange tomatoes on a platter and chill.

30 Minutes Before Serving
Set oven very hot (230°C, Mark 8, 450°F) or pre-heat grill for angels and devils on horseback.

15 Minutes Before Serving
Grill or bake devils and angels on horseback in heated oven; spear with toothpicks and keep warm.

During the Party
Fry shrimp toasts and serve at once.
Fry cheese balls, spear with toothpicks, and serve at once.

Assorted Cheese Pastries

For the pastry dough
450 g/1 lb/3 cups flour
1 tsp salt
225 g/$\frac{1}{2}$ lb/1 cup cooking fat
100 g/$\frac{1}{4}$ lb/1 cup grated dry Cheddar
  cheese
5–6 tbs water
1 egg beaten with 1 tsp salt (for glaze)

This quantity of dough is enough for two of the four fillings described below, and will make sufficient pastries for a party of fifty if you are serving all the other hot and cold canapés in the quantities suggested in this menu. If you want to make additional pastries, make the dough in 2 batches. The finished pastries freeze well, baked or un-baked.

Sift the flour with the salt into a bowl. Add the fat and cut with a pastry cutter or 2 knives into very small pieces. *Do not use your fingers or the dough will be sticky*. Stir in the cheese with just enough water to make a stiff dough. Knead very lightly until the pastry comes together; wrap and chill at least 1 hour.

Set the oven at moderately hot (190°C, Mark 5, 375°F). Divide the dough in half and roll out and shape each half, as described below, choosing 2 of the 4 fillings. Transfer to a baking sheet, and chill 15 minutes. Bake in the heated oven 15 minutes for the anchovy fingers, sausage rolls, and anchovy diamonds and 10–12 minutes for the cheese fingers or until golden brown. Transfer to a rack to cool. *You can make the pastries up to 48 hours ahead and keep them in an airtight container, or they can be frozen.*

For serving, arrange them in neat rows on a silver platter.

Anchovy Fingers

Roll out the dough to a strip 20 cm/8 inches wide and 46 cm/18 inches long and cut it in half lengthwise. Brush one half with egg glaze and lay 2 tins anchovy fillets, drained, crosswise on it at 2-cm/$\frac{3}{4}$-inch intervals. Place the second rectangle on top and press down with a finger between each fillet to outline the anchovies. Brush with egg glaze and cut into fingers between the anchovies. Makes about 22 fingers.

Cheese Fingers

Roll out the dough to a strip 20 cm/8 inches wide and 46 cm/18 inches long and brush with egg glaze. Sprinkle thickly with 4 tbs grated Parmesan cheese. Cut in half lengthwise, trim the edges and cut cross-wise into fingers 2 cm/$\frac{3}{4}$ inch wide and 10 cm/4 inches long. Makes about 44 fingers.

Sausage Rolls

Roll out the dough to a strip 20 cm/8 inches wide and 46 cm/18 inches long, brush with egg glaze, and cut in 3 length-wise, trimming the edges. Lay 700 g/ 1½ pounds baby chipolata sausages along one edge of each strip and roll them up to enclose the sausages. Press gently to seal, with the seam underneath, and cut the roll between each sausage. Brush them with egg glaze. Makes about 28 rolls.

Anchovy Diamonds

Roll the dough to a 20 cm × 41 cm/8 × 16 inch rectangle and cut it in half to form 2 squares. Spread 1 square with a 5-cm/2-ounce tube of anchovy paste; set the other square on top and press lightly. Chill 15 minutes, brush with egg glaze, cut into 4-cm/1½-inch strips, then crosswise into diamonds. Makes about 30 diamonds.

Smoked Salmon Rolls

1 loaf unsliced whole wheat bread
100 g/¼ lb/½ cup butter, softened
450 g/1 lb smoked salmon, very thinly sliced
freshly ground black pepper
juice 2–3 lemons
little cayenne (optional)

These rolls can be made ahead and kept in the refrigerator for a day, or they can be frozen for 1–2 weeks. This quantity makes 40–50 rolls and you can easily increase or decrease it.

Cut all but the 2 side crusts off the bread and freeze it until hard. *Freezing makes it easier to slice.* Spread one end of the loaf with softened butter and slice it as thinly as possible, spreading each slice with butter before cutting it. Trim the remaining crusts and cover each slice of bread with smoked salmon. Sprinkle with black pepper, lemon juice, and a little cayenne, if you like, and roll up the slices as tightly as possible; keep them tightly wrapped in the refrigerator, or freeze.

To serve: Let the rolls come to room temperature and arrange them on a silver platter.

Stuffed Tomatoes

2–3 lb tiny tomatoes
salt and freshly ground black pepper

For filling
1 jar (80 g/3¾ oz) lumpfish caviar
175 g/6 oz cream cheese
3–4 tbs cream

icing bag and small star nozzle (optional)

The flavour of the finest malassol caviar
would be lost in the tomatoes, but if you
are feeling extravagant, try crushed caviar
at a quarter the price. Otherwise black
lumpfish caviar is quite acceptable for this
recipe.

Cut a lid from the rounded end of the tomatoes and scoop out half the seeds with a
coffee spoon. Sprinkle all of them inside
with pepper and half of them with salt;
*tomatoes stuffed with caviar do not need any
salt.* Fill the caviar into the unsalted tomatoes using 2 small spoons. Soften the
cream cheese with enough cream to make a
mixture that pipes easily, and put it in an
icing bag fitted with a small star nozzle. Fill
the remaining tomatoes with cheese. Alternatively, the tomatoes can be filled using a
teaspoon. *You can prepare 12 hours ahead up
to this point.* Chill the tomatoes until the
cheese is firm, then cover them and keep in
the refrigerator.
    To serve: Arrange the tomatoes in a
checkerboard pattern on a silver platter.

Devils on Horseback

450 g/1 lb sliced bacon
450 g/1 lb chicken livers, cut in 2–3 pieces
    or 450 g/1 lb stoned prunes

toothpicks; 5–6 skewers

This recipe makes about 50 devils, and you
can easily make more or less. When cooked,
they can be kept warm for up to 20 minutes
without harm.

Cut the bacon slices in half and roll each
piece around a piece of chicken liver or a
prune. Thread the rolls on skewers (this
makes them easy to turn during cooking).
*You can prepare 12 hours ahead up to this
point.* Keep the rolls, covered, in the refrigerator.
    A short time before serving, set the rolls
on a rack and grill 3–4 minutes on each
side until the bacon is brown and crisp, or
bake them in a very hot oven (230°C, Mark
8, 450°F) for about 10 minutes on each
side. Drain on paper towels, spear each
devil on a toothpick, and serve on a silver
platter lined with a white napkin.

Angels on Horseback

Follow the recipe for devils on horseback,
but substitute 1 kg/2 lb standard oysters,
drained, for the chicken livers. Makes 50
angels.

Shrimp Toasts

450g/1 lb raw shrimps, peeled
1 tin (225 g/$\frac{1}{2}$ lb) water chestnuts, drained
2 tsp chopped fresh ginger root
2 eggs, beaten to mix
1 tbs cornflour
1 tbs sherry
salt and pepper
10–12 slices white bread, crusts removed
deep fat (for frying)

This quantity makes 80 toasts and the recipe can be doubled or halved. It is also a delicious appetizer, but cut the bread in half instead of in four as for these canapés.

Mix the shrimps, water chestnuts, and ginger root, and work the mixture, a little at a time, in a blender. Put in a bowl and stir in the eggs, cornflour, sherry, and salt and pepper to taste. Dip a knife in water to prevent sticking and spread the shrimp mixture on the bread; cut each slice in four squares. *You can prepare 12 hours ahead up to this point.* Keep the toasts, tightly covered, in the refrigerator.

    A short time before serving, heat the fat to 190°C, Mark 5, 375°F on a fat thermometer (a piece of bread will brown in 10 seconds). Lower a few of the toasts, shrimp side down, into the fat, dropping them from a height of about 2$\frac{1}{2}$ cm/1 inch. Fry until the bread is golden, lift out and drain on paper towels. Keep them warm in a low oven with the door open while frying the remaining toasts. Serve on a silver platter lined with a white napkin.

Cheese Dreams

50 g/2 oz/$\frac{2}{3}$ cup Parmesan cheese
2 egg whites
$\frac{1}{4}$ tsp mustard
freshly ground black pepper
deep fat (for frying)

toothpicks

If possible, these balls should be served at once, as they deflate on standing. This quan ity makes about 25 balls; you can easily double it.

Beat the cheese into the egg white to make a mixture that just falls from the spoon. Beat in the mustard and pepper to taste. *You can prepare 24 hours ahead up to this point.* Keep the mixture covered in the refrigerator.

    A short time before serving, heat the deep fat to 190°C, Mark 5, 375°F on a fat thermometer (a piece of bread will brown in 10 seconds). Using two teaspoons, drop teaspoonsful of the mixture into the hot fat and fry them, a few at a time, until puffed and golden brown. Lift out, drain them on paper towels, and keep warm in a low oven with the door open while frying the remaining mixture. Spear the balls with toothpicks and serve on a silver platter lined with a white napkin.

Single-Plate Supper

Oxtail Soup
Cornish Pasties
Spiced Fruitcake
Cheese

Among soup bones used for stock none is so rich as the neglected oxtail, the tail of the beef steer. The bones are full of gelatine, and after five or more hours of simmering, the soup acquires a wonderful glossy brown colour. Oxtail soup is best made ahead because the flavour improves on standing and at the same time you will have a chance to chill it thoroughly to skim the layer of fat which rises to the surface of the soup and solidifies. To transform the soup into a party

dish, add a spoon of sherry or Madeira to each bowl or mug before serving.

Cornish pasties are a very old favourite snack or supper dish. These pastry turn-overs were made for Cornish tin miners to carry underground to their work. Unlike the usual turnover, which is a circle of dough folded in half and sealed on the crescent edge, a pasty is oval, like a pouch, with the dough drawn up over the filling and sealed at the top. Originally one half of the pasty was filled with meat and the other with fruit of some kind, so it was a main course and dessert all in one. Today pasties have a savoury filling of meat, usually a less expensive cut of steak such as top rump or topside, to which you add diced root vegetables like carrots, potatoes, celery, and turnip.

The habit of eating a fruitcake or fruit pie with cheese is a North Country one. This spiced fruitcake is very light, made with two kinds of raisins and baked in a loaf pan for easy slicing. Wedges of mild Cheddar cheese or Wensleydale would be its best match.

This single-plate supper avoids most of the problems of large-scale cooking. Few big pans are needed, and one burner and one oven are enough both for cooking and any reheating. This is one occasion when paper plates and cups (for the soup, get the jumbo size) are indicated, and the many colourful designs now available are worth the extra pennies. The menu would be ideal for a fund-raising affair. The components are inexpensive while avoiding the usual budget stand-bys of meatloaf and macaroni and cheese.

COUNTDOWN

1–2 Weeks Before
Make 2 batches of fruitcakes and store in
   airtight containers.

2–3 Days Before
Make oxtail soup and cover.

Day Before
Make Cornish pasties and keep tightly
   covered.

In the Morning
Skim fat from soup.
Slice cakes and cover.
Slice cheese.

1 Hour Before Serving
Set oven at low (150°C, Mark 2, 300°F).

30 Minutes Before Serving
Reheat soup.
Heat Cornish pasties in oven.

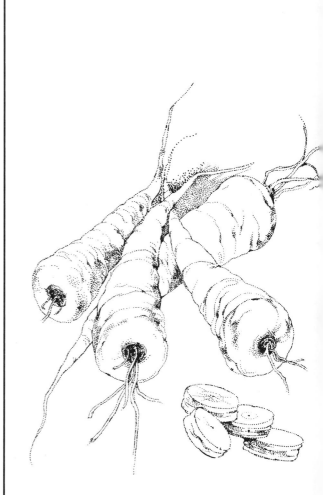

Oxtail Soup

2.5 dl/$\frac{1}{2}$ pt/1 cup oil
12 oxtails (about 8 kg/18 lb), cut in 5-cm/2-
   inch pieces
20 medium onions, chopped
8 carrots, chopped
small bunch celery, chopped
100 g/$\frac{1}{4}$ lb/1 cup flour
6 l/12 pt beef stock
1 kg/2 lb tinned tomatoes, chopped (juice
   reserved)
9 l/4$\frac{1}{2}$ pt water
10 cloves garlic, crushed
2 tbs thyme
10 bay leaves
bunch parsley
salt and freshly ground black pepper

You can halve this recipe; any left over
freezes well, so you can keep it for another
occasion.

In 2 large casseroles or soup kettles, heat
the oil and brown the pieces of oxtail very
well on all sides. *This adds a great deal of
flavour to the soup.* Take out and drain off all
but about 4 tablespoons fat from each pan.
Add the onions, carrots, and celery, and
cook gently until soft but not brown. Add
the flour and cook, stirring occasionally,
until both flour and vegetables are
browned. Add the stock, tomatoes and their
juice, water, garlic, thyme, bay leaves and
parsley tied together with string, and salt
and pepper. Bring to the boil, replace the
oxtail pieces; cover and simmer over very
low heat for about 5 hours, stirring occasionally and adding more water if the liquid
evaporates rapidly. At the end of cooking
the soup should be rich and the meat falling
off the bones.

Let the soup cool to tepid, then lift out
the pieces of oxtail and remove the meat,
discarding the bones and fat. Chop the meat
and return it to the pan. Simmer 30
minutes longer, then discard the bay leaves
and parsley and taste for seasoning. *You can
prepare at least 12 hours or up to 3 days ahead
to this point.* Keep the soup covered, in the
refrigerator. *Do not leave it in an aluminium
pan or it will taste metallic.*

Before serving, skim the solidified fat from
the surface of the soup and bring it to the
boil. It can be kept hot for an hour or more
without harm.

Cornish Pasties

1½ kg/3 lb lean topside or top rump of beef,
 cut in 1-cm/⅜-inch cubes
5 medium onions, chopped
6 medium potatoes, peeled and diced
6 carrots, peeled and diced
3 medium turnips, peeled and diced
½ small bunch celery, diced
1 tbs thyme, oregano, or rosemary
 (optional)
2 tbs chopped parsley
salt and freshly ground black pepper
2 eggs, beaten to mix with 2 tsp salt (for
 glaze)

For half quantity of pastry
1.35 kg/3 lb flour
1 tbs salt
350 g/¾ lb/1½ cups cooking fat
350 g/¾ lb/1½ cups butter
3.25 dl/¾ pt/1½–2 cups cold water
6 egg yolks

It is impossible to make enough pastry for
50 pasties all at once, so you will need to
make 2 batches of the above quantity. The
filling is enough for 50 pasties. You can
easily halve or quarter the recipe.

For the pastry: Sift the flour into a bowl
with the salt, add the cooking fat and butter
and cut into small pieces with a pastry cutter or two knives. Rub in with the fingertips until the mixture resembles crumbs.
With a knife stir in 3.25 dl/¾ pt/1½ cups
water mixed with the egg yolks, then knead
lightly with your hand, adding more water
if necessary to make a dough that is soft
but not sticky. Wrap tightly and chill 30
minutes. Make the second batch of dough
in the same way.

For the filling: Mix the beef with the onions,
potatoes, carrots, turnips, celery, thyme,
oregano, or rosemary (if used), parsley and
plenty of salt and pepper. Divide one batch
of dough in half and roll out to ½ cm/
¼ inch thickness. Cut out twelve 17 cm/
6½-inch rounds using a plate or pan lid as a
guide and pile about 125 g/4 oz/½ cup filling
down the centre of each one. Brush the
edges with glaze. Bring two opposite edges
together over the top of the filling and
pinch them to seal. Flute the edges to form
a ridge along the top; brush the pasties
with egg glaze. Transfer them to a baking
sheet, cover, and chill thoroughly. Shape
and chill remaining pasties in the same
way. Set oven to hot (200°C, Mark 6,
400°F).

 Bake the pasties in the heated oven for
15–20 minutes or until lightly browned.
Turn down the heat to moderate (180°C,
Mark 4, 350°F) and continue baking 20–25
minutes or until meat and vegetables are
tender when the pasties are tested with a
skewer. If they brown too much before the
end of cooking, cover them with foil. Transfer them to a rack to cool. You can prepare
the pasties 24 hours ahead and keep them,
tightly covered, in the refrigerator. They
also freeze well.

 A short time before serving, warm the
pasties in a low oven (150°C, Mark 2,
300°F) for 25–30 minutes, or until a skewer
inserted in the centre for ½ minute is hot to
the touch when withdrawn.

Spiced Fruit Cake

$\frac{3}{4}$ l/1$\frac{1}{4}$ pt/4 cups boiling water
450 g/1 lb/4 cups raisins
225 g/$\frac{1}{2}$ lb/1$\frac{1}{2}$ cups sultanas
175 g/6 oz/1$\frac{1}{2}$ cups coarsely chopped
  walnuts
675 g/1$\frac{1}{2}$ lb/6 cups flour
1 tbs bicarbonate of soda
2 tsp baking powder
1 tsp salt
450 g/1 lb/2 cups fat
1 kg/2 lb/4 cups sugar
4 tsp vanilla extract
juice 1 lemon
4 eggs
4 egg yolks
1 tbs ground cinnamon
2 tsp ground allspice
2 tsp ground nutmeg

four 23 × 13 × 8 cm/9 × 5 × 3 inch loaf pans

This quantity of cake must be made in 2 batches because the batter is hard to handle. The flavour improves if you store the cakes in an airtight container for 1–2 weeks.

Grease the loaf pans; line each with a piece of greaseproof paper and grease the paper. Set the oven at moderately low (170°C, Mark 3, 325°F). Pour boiling water over both kinds of raisins and the walnuts, stir well and let cool. Drain off the liquid just before use and divide the mixture in half.

Sift 350 g/$\frac{3}{4}$ lb/3 cups flour with 1$\frac{1}{2}$ teaspoons bicarbonate of soda, 1 teaspoon baking powder and $\frac{1}{2}$ teaspoon salt. Cream 225 g/$\frac{1}{2}$ lb/1 cup fat, gradually beat in 450 g/1 lb/2 cups sugar and continue beating until light and fluffy. Stir in 2 teaspoons vanilla and half the lemon juice. Beat 2 eggs and 2 egg yolks with 1$\frac{1}{2}$ teaspoons cinnamon and 1 teaspoon each of allspice and nutmeg until slightly thick. Beat into the sugar mixture, a little at a time. Stir in the flour alternately with one portion of raisins and nuts, starting and ending with the flour. Spoon the batter into 2 of the prepared pans and bake in the heated oven for 1$\frac{1}{2}$ hours or until a skewer inserted in the centre comes out clean. Let cool in the pan until tepid, then turn out on a rack to cool completely. Make and bake the remaining batter in the same way. Store the cakes in an airtight container for 1–2 weeks.

SOME COOKING TECHNIQUES

To Peel Tomatoes

Many Tomatoes: Pour boiling water over
the tomatoes in a bowl, let stand 10 seconds
and drain. This cooks the tomatoes slightly
and loosens the skins, which peel off easily.
If the tomatoes are underripe, 15 seconds
soaking may be needed, but do not leave
them too long or the surface will be soft.
One or two Tomatoes: Spear the tomato on
a two-pronged fork and hold in a gas flame,
turning until the skin blisters and bursts;
take from the heat and peel.

To Seed Tomatoes

When Chopping Tomatoes: Discard core
and cut in half crosswise. Hold tomato half
in the hollow of the hand and squeeze
firmly to force out the seeds, then chop.
When Cutting Tomatoes in Strips: Discard
core and cut in quarters through the core.
Cut each quarter in half or four and discard
the seeds from each strip.

To Peel and Core Pineapples

Cut the plume and the bottom from the
pineapple with a large knife. Look at the
pineapple skin and trace the lines of eyes
which twist around the fruit from top to
bottom. With a small pointed knife, cut
along one of these lines of eyes, slanting the
knife inwards at a 45-degree angle. Cut
along the other side of the same line of
eyes, slanting the knife in the opposite
direction so the cuts meet in the middle
under the eyes. Lift out and discard the line
of eyes. Repeat until all the peel has been
removed. With an apple corer, cut the core
from the pineapple. Slice the fruit or cut it
in chunks as called for in the recipe. The
slices will have a scalloped edge where the
eyes were removed.

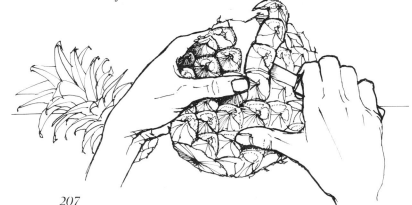

207

To Peel and Stone Peaches

Pour boiling water over the peaches, let stand 10–20 seconds, depending on ripeness, and drain. Cut peaches in half, running the knife through the indentation on one side, and twist each half sharply to loosen from the stone. Discard the stone, then peel the peach halves.

Note: Peaches are difficult to peel if they are unripe.

To Whisk Egg Whites in a Copper Bowl

Clean the bowl by rubbing the surface with 1–2 tablespoons salt and 1–2 tablespoons vinegar or the cut edge of a lemon. Rinse and dry thoroughly – the surface of the copper will be shining and almost pink in colour. The copper bowl must be cleaned every time it is used. Add the egg whites; they should be at room temperature. To whip properly, egg whites, bowl, and whisk must be completely free of any trace of water, grease, or egg yolk. With a large balloon whisk, start beating the egg whites, working at first in the bottom of the bowl and lifting the whisk high in a circle to beat in as much air as possible. As the whites break up and become frothy, increase the size of the circles until you are using the whole bowl and whisking as fast as possible, still lifting the whisk out of the bowl. When the egg whites are quite stiff, change the motion by whisking in large circles as fast as possible with the whisk always down in the egg whites, in contact with the bowl. This stiffens the whites, rather than beating air into them. Continue for 1–2 minutes until the egg whites form only a shallow peak when the whisk is lifted. When a copper bowl is used, the volume of the whites is greater than with a regular beater.

To Truss a Chicken, Duck, or Pigeon

Thread a trussing needle with thin string. Set the bird on its back on a board and push the legs well back and down toward the board. Insert the needle through the leg joint to catch back one leg, pass the needle through the bird and catch the other leg on the other side. Twist the wing pinions under the bird, if possible catching the neck skin underneath them. Insert the needle into one wing (leaving a stitch of string leading from the leg) then under the backbone of the bird and out the other side, catching the other wing. Tie the ends of string from the leg and wing tightly together at the side. Tuck the parson's nose up into the cavity of the bird. Rethread the

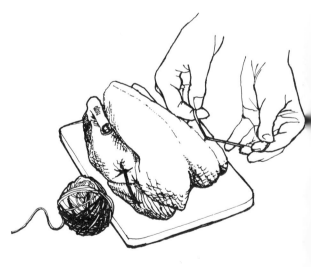

trussing needle and run it through the rear of the bird to hold down the nose, then insert the needle through the end of both drumsticks. Tie the loose ends tightly together.

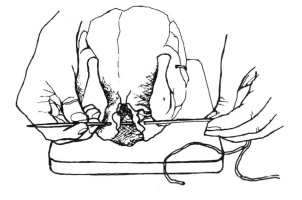

To Cut Up Raw or Cooked Chicken

With a sharp knife, cut down between leg and body at the leg joint. Twist the leg sharply out to break the joint, cut through it and pull the leg from the body; trim the drumstick knuckle with poultry shears. Repeat with other leg. Hold the knife at the end of the breastbone, where the breastbone and wishbone meet, and cut down to the wing joint, parallel to one side of the wishbone. Cut through the wing joint; in this way a portion of the breast is cut off with the wing. Repeat on the other side. With poultry shears or scissors, cut away backbone and ribs, leaving the breast. Cut the breast in half with the shears to make 6 pieces of chicken. If 8 pieces are called for, cut the leg in two through the thigh joint.

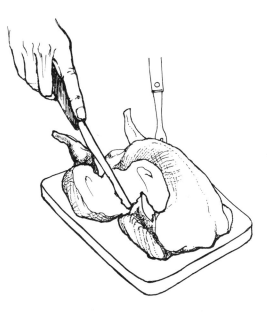

To Lard Meat

Cut fresh pork fat or bacon into strips 8–10 cm/3–4 inches long and ½ cm/¼ inch wide. Thread the strips into a larding needle and thread the strips of fat or bacon into the meat, working across the grain. Some larding needles have a channel to enclose the fat; others have a spring at one end to catch the end of the fat. Meat can also be larded with flavourings such as ham, tongue, and pieces of truffle. Good butchers will lard meat for you.

To Bard Meat

Wrap the meat in a very thin layer of pork fat, then tie it with string. This is usually done by the butcher who prepares the roast. Fat for barding is obtainable from some butchers.

To Make Simple Stock

Stock is made by simmering meat, poultry, or fish bones and vegetables in water until all the flavour is extracted. The bones may be raw or cooked, and any leftover bones from a roast can be used, providing they are trimmed of fat; the vegetables should be uncooked. Beef stock is full flavoured; chicken and veal are lighter and duck stock is particularly rich. Stock can be kept for up to 3 days in the refrigerator. If storing longer, bring the stock to the boil, simmer 10 minutes, and chill again. It can be frozen.

For beef stock, using raw bones, roast them with quartered carrots and quartered, unpeeled onions (the peel adds colour to the stock) in a very hot oven (230°C, Mark 8, 450°F) for ½–¾ hour or until thoroughly browned. If using cooked beef bones, do not brown them. Put the bones and vegetables in a large pan with a few peppercorns, a very little salt, and water to cover. Add a lid, bring slowly to the boil and skim. Simmer, skimming occasionally, for at least 3 hours, adding more water if it evaporates rapidly. Strain the stock; chill and skim off any solidified fat.

Veal stock: Follow the instructions for beef stock, but use raw bones and do not brown them.

Chicken and duck stock: Follow the instructions for beef stock, but if using raw bones do not brown them. Simmer the stock only 1½–2 hours.

Mixed stock: Good stock can also be made from any mixture of meat or poultry bones available, with vegetables added.

INDEX